Good Deeds in Old Age

Good Deeds in Old Age

Volunteering by the New Leisure Class

Susan Maizel Chambré
Baruch College

Lexington Books
D.C. Heath and Company/Lexington, Massachusetts/Toronto

Library of Congress Cataloging-in-Publication Data

Chambré, Susan Maizel.
    Good deeds in old age.

    Includes index.
    Voluntarism—United States. 2. Aged volunteers—United States. I. Title.
HN90.V64C48   1987   361.3'7'0880565   86-45055
ISBN 0-669-13091-5 (alk. paper)

Published simultaneously in Canada
Printed in the United States of America
Casebound International Standard Book Number: 0-669-13091-5
Library of Congress Catalog Card Number: 86-45055

The paper used in this publication meets the minimum requirements of American National
Standard for Information Sciences—Permanence of Paper for Printed Library Materials,
ANSI Z39.48-1984.

87 88 89 90 8 7 6 5 4 3 2 1

In memory of my grandmother, Meryl Maizel,
who gave of her time and of herself to her landsleit.

Contents

Figures and Tables

Figures

Tables

Foreword

Otto Pollak, Professor Emeritus
Department of Sociology, University of Pennsylvania

At the "old, old" age of 78 years, I was asked by my former student to write a foreword to a book on an unfamiliar topic, volunteering by the elderly. On the other hand, I have a high degree of preparation for this task since my first published paper, done while I was a graduate student at the University of Pennsylvania in 1941, dealt with the subject of criminality in old age. Since then, I have been an active participant in the development of the literature of social gerontology and have continued to closely follow its development during my semiretirement. I have found it a challenge and a reward to respond to Professor Susan Maizel Chambré's request to introduce her book with my impressions of its value and contribution to the field at the present time.

As a professor, I naturally looked first at the author's acquaintance with the pertinent literature and must immediately record my admiration for the amount of spade work that Professor Chambré has done in covering the publications related to her topic. The intensity and at the same time gentle handling of the mountain of pertinent publications will make her book a veritable bibliography of material on volunteering in old age. In a period of history where publishing has become an academic career requirement and a support of one's scholarly self-image, the amount of available literature on almost any topic becomes an impediment rather than a resource for further work. Professor Chambré has conquered this difficulty with admirable industry and success.

The second and perhaps more relevant contribution of her book is its statistical basis for supporting the validity of the continuity theory of adjustment in old age. This is probably a greater contribution to social gerontology than her other findings although it is less immediately related to the issue of volunteering as a role substitute. In a cultural climate that extolls activity as a virtue and a therapy this cannot have been an easy task. It required objectivity and demonstrates a liberation from cultural bias and the ability to use statistics as a tool rather than as a weapon in the evaluation of divergent theories. Step by step the role of social variables which seem to be connected with degrees of volunteering by people in advancing years are presented, leading to plausible answers on the propensities of various population groups for volunteering. The author is then inventive and practical in her recommendations for increasing recruitment of volunteers and discusses this problem in the context of demographic and social changes.

To her penetrating analysis, I would like to add an addendum based on personal experience which might not be generalized but is worth mentioning. Old people do not derive as much free time from retirement as is so frequently assumed. The aging body takes more time for every item of activity. The role of chronic patient with relentless harassment by regular health check-ups makes so many time demands on aging persons that life maintenance leaves many fewer empty hours than is generally assumed.

Preface

A s I move toward the fifth decade of my life, writing this book has led me to speculate about how I will construct a meaningful existence when I too begin to experience significant "role losses," a decline in my physical strength, and a shrinking of my social network.

This book began as an investigation of a fairly straightforward issue: the social characteristics associated with whether or not older people were involved in doing volunteer work. Even before I started the formal work on this project, I had already found, using another data source, that a fairly logical conclusion would probably not be supported by the data: the people who would theoretically have the greatest amount of free time—people with fewer work and family responsibilities—would not be the ones who were most often involved in doing volunteer work.

In order to try to understand this finding and to create, first, a report and, then, a book that would splice together existing information and the results of my own data analysis, I delved into virtually the entire range of findings in the field of social gerontology. It became clear to me that volunteering by some older people is part of a larger pattern of social relationships. Older volunteers are more actively involved in a number of different sorts of activities: reading, going to restaurants, walking, and exercising. They also have stronger family ties and go to church or to synagogue more regularly. To some extent, this is related to their economic situation. Volunteers are a more affluent portion of the older population. They can afford to pay for the transportation and the clothing that might be necessary for volunteering. In addition, the people who volunteer are the better-educated segment of the older population, a group that also has prestige or the tangible job skills which make them attractive to organizations.

The goal of social science is to describe reality and to provide explanations for relationships among variables. Just as it is important to understand how volunteering is part of a life-style of some older people, so too is it valuable for a book such as this to provide professionals working with older people, with volunteers—especially older volunteers—with some guidelines on how to nurture and to expand volunteering by older people.

Just twenty years ago, two articles published in major professional journals were skeptical about the potential involvement of older people in volunteer work. The authors wondered if older people were really interested in doing volunteer work and if organizations would employ them. How far we have come. Older people now play a vital role as volunteers. Yet, compare the amount of time older people spend as volunteers with the amount of time spent watching television. It is my hope that this book will shed some light on this subject so that more older people can see volunteering as a viable way to achieve meaning in their own lives and, at the same time, make a contribution and feel a stronger connection to the life of their society.

Acknowledgments

A number of institutions and individuals provided me with assistance and support during the course of writing this book. I owe a great deal to all of them, and I hope that these words of appreciation will be a sufficient expression of my gratitude.

The American Association of Retired Persons (AARP) Andrus Foundation provided generous financial support to a novice researcher in the field of gerontology. This support freed me from teaching responsibilities and provided me with resources that would not have otherwise been available. I hope that the findings of this book will be valuable to the staff of the AARP and also to the several million members of this important organization.

My home institution, Baruch College, extended direct and indirect support in several ways. The college's Center for the Study of Business and Government provided me with released time at several phases of the project and enabled me to transform a raw report to the Andrus Foundation into a more polished book. I would particularly like to thank Harold Hochman, former director of the center, who arranged for my affiliation with the center and who encouraged me to begin the project and to apply for my first grant. The released time provided by the center was especially needed at a time when I was consolidating my career and expanding my family. Edward Saueracker, former assistant director of the center, was extremely helpful at all stages, ably serving as the administrator of this project and ensuring that staffing and budgetary matters were in order. Several other staff members at the center—Rose Santoro, Donna Lambert, Susan Massaro, and Eva Mattina—provided secretarial support.

Baruch assisted me in several other ways. Funds from the Scholar Assistance Program helped me to purchase a microcomputer which was used to revise and complete the final manuscript. I made extensive use of a number of services of the Baruch library: bibliographic searches, interlibrary loans, and the article-alert service. The Educational Computer Center provided me with funds and with a great deal of technical assistance.

In addition to institutional support, I received assistance from a number of colleagues and friends at Baruch. Norman W. Storer has been a mentor to me providing advice and counsel as well as a careful editing of an early draft of the manuscript. Ginny Lotz has been both a secretary and a sounding board in my home department. My thanks also to Howard Negrin, Ida Lowe, Erich Neubacher, Joanne D'Antonio (who was a superb research assistant), and especially Sherry Prupis of the Educational Computer Center, who provided a great deal of technical and substantive advice.

Throughout my professional career, I have received ongoing intellectual and emotional support from my study group. I wish to express my thanks and appreciation to Carol Poll Aronson, Dorothy Jones Jessup, Natalie Hannon, Corinne Kirchner, and Miriam Sudit.

This work was done at a time of my life when I was establishing myself on two fronts: career and family. My husband, Bob, has done more than help. He has shared so many of the practical and emotional tasks associated with running a complex household with four young children. My parents, Norman and Lucille Maizel, have been important to us as well. I want to thank them for always being there to help us pursue our dreams.

But one whose good deeds exceed his wisdom, to what is he likened? To a tree whose branches are few but whose roots are numerous; even if all the winds in the world were to come and blow against it, they could not budge it from its place; as it is said: "And he shall be like a tree planted by waters, toward the stream spreading its roots, and it shall not notice the heat's arrival, and its foliage shall be fresh; in the year of drought it shall not worry, nor shall it cease from yielding fruit."

Sayings of the Fathers

1
The Role of Volunteering in Older People's Lives: Role Substitute and Leisure Activity

Several historical trends have converged to create a new leisure class, older people. The development of public and private pension programs in the United States over the past fifty years has freed many older people from the necessity of earning a living. These programs have also improved their economic status, so more of them are economically independent than in the past.[1] At the same time, these programs have either permitted, motivated, or even forced older people to leave the labor force. The freedom from having to earn a living and the expansion of retirement, combined with the limited family responsibilities of older people, have created a sizeable—and growing—leisure class.

There were about 9 million people over the age of sixty-five in 1940, when the first Social Security checks were distributed. This was about 7 percent of the U.S. population. This number had tripled by 1983, when there were 27.5 million older people, 11.7 percent of the population.[2] One estimate projects that this proportion will rise to about 17 percent in the year 2020.[3]

The trends toward early retirement—the typical worker in the United States now retires at the age of 62[4]—and increased longevity have expanded the number of years and the proportion of people's lives spent in retirement. A study of historical changes in life expectancy and retirement found that the typical American man lived to be 48 years of age in 1900, and, on average, spent 6.5 percent of his life in retirement. By 1980, a man could expect to live about twenty years longer and spend close to 17 percent of his life in retirement.[5]

There are several important consequences of these changes. The first is economic. Since there are currently 30 "nonworkers" over 60 for every 100 wage earners who are between ages 20 and 59,[6] there is a great deal of public concern about whether or not the Social Security system will be financially viable in the future. A second implication is that there are more and more older people who have limited work and family responsibilities. Despite the fact that there is a great deal of excellent research in the field of social gerontology, little is known about how some older people lead meaningful lives in the context of a work-oriented society that either encourages or forces them to retire, and where they have relatively limited family responsibilities.

Virtually all societies make distinctions between people on the basis of their age. Because they are thought to have different capabilities, young people and old people are typically assigned to different tasks in most societies. Thus, the social roles available to people differ over the life cycle. The way people allocate their time is determined by work and family responsibilities during most of their lives. Children spend time in school; adults are involved with their work, their marriages, and their parental responsibilities. The time left over after this is "leisure"; the amount of leisure time available changes over the life cycle and the kinds of choices that people make about how to spend their time also vary at different stages in their lives.

In American society, the demands of work and family life shift dramatically in old age. Retirement, widowhood, and reduced parental responsibilities alter the external constraints that influence how people allocate their time. In both subjective as well as objective fashions, people's lives begin to change dramatically in the seventh decade of life. They face retirement; they might experience the death of a spouse; they have less energy or may even have problems with their health; friends and relatives migrate to other areas of the country or die; and children move or place fewer demands on their parents.

A major question facing Americans both individually and collectively is whether a sizeable proportion of a population living in a work-oriented society can lead meaningful lives while, at the same time, lacking significant work or family obligations. Volunteering is often viewed as a way older people can maintain or acquire an added dimension to their lives.

The Place of Volunteering in Older People's Lives

A substantial number of older people are involved in doing volunteer work. In 1981, almost one fourth of people 65 or older, or 5.9 million people, spent some time working without pay for a variety of organizations and institutions.[7] When volunteering is defined more broadly as "working in some way to help others for no monetary pay," even more are categorized as volunteers—37 percent of them or about 9.5 million.[8]

A number of programs developed during the past decade have been designed to expand volunteering by senior citizens. Older volunteers are viewed as a valuable resource; they are seen as a reliable and experienced labor pool. This is a relatively recent situation and represents a very distinctive shift in attitudes. Two articles published about twenty years ago identified some significant barriers to volunteering by older people, namely older people's lack of interest and the unwillingness of organizations to accept and to employ older people as volunteers.[9]

These are no longer serious concerns. Older people are seen as a valuable source of unpaid labor who are able to transfer professional skills and life experience to their work.[10] Not only have the perceptions of older volunteers changed, they have become even more crucial because the traditional type of volunteer who is available during daytime hours—homemakers without young children—is relatively fewer in number because more and more women are in the paid labor force.

Current programs designed for older people—such as the Foster Grandparent Program, the Retired Senior Volunteer Program (RSVP), and the Service Corps of Retired Executives (SCORE) (which are sponsored by the federal government) as well as a host of private programs—have greatly expanded the settings where older volunteers work as well as the types of jobs they perform. Older volunteers work with potential child abusers as well as with abused and neglected children,[11] in day care centers,[12] and in schools.[13] Programs for foster grandparents have them visiting prison inmates,[14] retarded children and adults, hospital patients,[15] as well as mental patients.[16] Other new roles include consulting with small business owners,[17] participating in VISTA and the Peace Corps,[18] and providing services to other older people in their own communities and also in nursing homes.[19]

These activities have clear social benefits and enhance people's lives in several ways since volunteering can simultaneously fulfill a number of motivations: to be altruistic, to achieve self-actualization, to gain political influence, and to find substitutes for work and family roles. There is a particular emphasis on the last of these, the role-loss function. Many discussions of the role of volunteering in the lives of older people stress that it is a way they can find role substitutes.[20] Like work, it provides the structure of a paid job: a place to go to and to dress for, the gratification derived from a job well done, and the basis for the social relationships in a work setting. Unlike work, however, volunteering is unpaid. For many people, this may be an important barrier since it is often believed that any job worth doing is one meriting payment.

Purpose of the Book

This book is a secondary analysis of data from a major survey of older people. The data collection was originally sponsored by the National Council on the Aging, and the interviews were conducted by Louis Harris and Associates, who wrote a final report.[21]

This book focuses on the following questions:

What social characteristics are associated with whether or not older people are involved in doing volunteer work?

Is volunteering a substitute for role loss in old age?

Do older volunteers tend to have different patterns of social and leisure activities than their counterparts who are not involved in volunteer work?

Does volunteering contribute to higher life satisfaction or are older volunteers a self-selective group composed of people who had relatively high levels of life satisfaction before they started to volunteer?

What is the relative importance of the factors that influence volunteer participation by older people?

What are the book's implications for designing and administering programs for older volunteers?

A great deal has been published on the subject of volunteering by older people over the past twenty years.[22] Much of it is based on the experiences of practitioners; a relatively small proportion of publications on the topic are based on empirical studies. Such studies serve an important function for they can look carefully at whether or not some of the generalizations based on practitioner's experiences and on the outcome of specific programs are, in fact, valid conclusions.

Even though they are relatively few in number, the empirical studies on the subject are generally well conceived. They examine a broad range of social characteristics, attitudes, and psychological attributes that are correlated with volunteer participation by older people and are therefore an excellent guide to many of the potential correlates of volunteering considered in this book.

Correlates of Volunteering by the Elderly

Most discussions of the place of volunteering in older people's lives focus on the fact that it is a role substitute—that people volunteer to compensate for the loss of work and family roles. Despite the fact that this view is a central one, there is actually limited empirical support for it. A widely cited study of one of the earliest senior volunteer programs, the SERVE program, is the first place where the role-loss function of volunteering was actually discussed. Several facts about the participants led to the conclusion that role loss was a major impetus to joining the program. More than half of the participants originally entered the program in order to increase their social contacts.[23] Two-thirds of them were unmarried, and more than nine in ten were not working.[24] Since this project was extensively cited in subsequent discussions of volunteering, it is likely that the prevailing view that volunteering is a role substitute stems from this study.

A secondary analysis of data from a nationwide survey sponsored by ACTION in 1974 includes the first systematic investigation of whether role loss is, in fact, closely associated with volunteering by older people. The study concluded that role loss was not a major factor in understanding volunteering. In fact, retirement was not associated with volunteering at all,[25] a finding consistent with several other studies looking at interest in doing volunteer work[26] as well as actual participation.[27] Two other measures of involvement in social roles—whether or not people were widowed or living alone—were also not associated with volunteering in the ACTION sample.

There is a considerable amount of research on the association between volunteering and a number of demographic and social characteristics. Some studies look at a different variable measuring volunteering: interest in doing volunteer work rather than actual participation.[29] Two types of samples have been used. Some analyses, like this one, look at a sample of older people and categorize the respondents into volunteers and nonvolunteers.[30] Others are based on two or more samples composed of a group of volunteers and one or more groups composed of nonvolunteers selected so that comparisons can be made.[31]

Regardless of the methodology and the nature of the study population, several relationships have consistently appeared in virtually all of the studies. First, increasing age is negatively associated with volunteering, and volunteering is positively associated with two measures of socioeconomic status, education and income.[32] Even though it is logical to assume that declining health has an adverse effect on participation, this supposition is not strongly supported by empirical data.

There is a fairly limited amount of research on the connection between volunteering and other types of social and leisure activities. Two studies, which used very different sorts of study populations, had similar results. One of them used applicants for public housing and the other drew upon senior center attendees. Both types of sample contained volunteers and nonvolunteers. When the two types (volunteers and nonvolunteers) were compared, the most important difference between them was the way they used their leisure time.[33] Volunteers were more socially active—they belonged to a larger number of voluntary associations, more frequently attended meetings, and derived greater amounts of satisfaction from their involvement. They also differed in the amount of free time they had and their ability to use it: volunteers had less time to spare and more easily found ways to fill whatever free time they did have.[34] Another study, which compared members of three types of leisure groups (participants in an RSVP program, in a recreational setting, and in a nutrition program) found that volunteers had higher levels of formal social participation, but that they had lower levels of informal social contacts; as a rule they had fewer friends and were less involved in informal social gatherings.[35]

A major shortcoming of previous studies of volunteering by the elderly is that several methodological limitations do not permit strong inferences to be made on the basis of their conclusions. The nature of the samples and their sizes limit the ability to generalize their findings to older people as a group. All of the studies that use multivariate analyses and look at the combined effects of several factors at once are based on relatively small samples composed of residents of perhaps one or two geographic areas.

The data analyses performed on large, representative samples are mainly two-way cross-tabulations between volunteer status and various social characteristics. Although helpful, two-way cross-tabulations do not adequately test for the fact that a relationship between two variables may be actually due to another factor. For example, if there is a positive relationship between being married and being healthy, this association could be due to the fact that married people are younger than people who are widowed. If this is true, then the original relationship between being married and being healthy is a spurious relationship.

This book synthesizes existing findings and then (in chapter 10) creates a model of volunteer participation by the elderly. It expands our knowledge of the correlates of volunteering inasmuch as a broader range of independent variables are used: measures of role loss, age and health status, demographic characteristics (gender, race, and religion), socioeconomic status, social activity, leisure, and life satisfaction.

Volunteering can be considered from several vantage points. First, it involves the contribution of work skills with no financial compensation. Because of this, it is a type of leisure activity. Since volunteering often occurs within the context of a voluntary association, it is probably closely linked to membership and participation in voluntary groups; however, the link between them has not been studied empirically. Another dimension of volunteering is that like any work activity, it fosters significant social interaction.

In the course of writing this book, it became clear that an understanding of the meaning of volunteer work required some attention to the more general issue of leisure time for older people: the meaning of leisure among the older population, the impact of retirement on leisure, and how older people spend their leisure time. These issues are described in order to frame the research questions in broader perspective.

Leisure Patterns of Older People

The Issue of Leisure in the Older Population

Leisure time is usually described as the time left over after various obligations have been fulfilled. Older people as a group have been described as a "leisure class."[36] In theory, they should have greater amounts of discretionary time than younger people because they are retired and because their family responsibilities are usually limited. Because older people are less constrained by work and family obligations than younger people, they can theoretically exercise a greater amount of choice about how they spend their time.[37] Social gerontologists describe older people as "roleless" because they have, in effect, lost some of the ways that they were tied to the social order during earlier periods of their lives because many of them have retired or have been widowed.[38] Participation in various types of leisure activities—including volunteering—is viewed as a way to find role substitutes to compensate for role losses in other areas of life.[39] Because older people have more leisure and can choose how to spend their time, social gerontologists have devoted a considerable amount of attention to studying the leisure activities of older people.

American culture places a great emphasis on the work ethic. Doing some form of work, be it paid work at a job or unpaid work in the home, is thought to be essential in order to lead a normal life.[40] Keeping busy and being active are central values;[41] people such as welfare recipients who do not conform to these values are stigmatized. Even though retirement and widowhood are socially accepted status transitions, a common theme in the gerontological literature is that older people's well-being is higher when they are more involved in the life of their community.

People who were over 60 in 1981 (the sampling frame for this book) were born before 1921 and grew up in a work-oriented society where people had significantly less time for leisure. Factory, mill, or mine workers worked 72 hours a week in the 1870s—a time when the grandparents of many of today's older people were reaching maturity.[42] The typical older person spent his or her early years during a time when the average work week was 50 hours.[43]

Retirement is also a relatively recent phenomenon. In 1890, 68 percent of men over the age of 65 were in the paid labor force. By 1950 (10 years after Social Security payments were first distributed), this had declined to 42 percent of men in that age group; it declined further to 16 percent in 1984.[44]

The meaning of volunteering itself has changed. In an historical study, Barry Karl points out that the use of the word *volunteer* with its present meaning did not evolve until the turn of this century. Until then, this term was only used to describe people who were involved in religious activities.[45]

The meaning of work in American culture plus the relative recency of extensive leisure time and of retirement itself have several implications for this book. The first is whether older people have developed a "leisure competence," a knowledge of the kinds of activities available and the ability to derive sufficient meaning from leisure to counterbalance other role losses.[46] Several observers have seriously questioned whether leisure activities can serve this purpose, do serve this purpose, and should serve this purpose.[47] A lack of specific responsibilities can be a source of embarrassment for a retired person, particularly if retirement occurred on an involuntary basis. For some people, leisure activities will not fill the gap and be a gratifying substitute for work. For others, retirement may not be so crucial because work may not have been so central to their lives.[48]

Also of interest are the questions of whether or not older people do, in fact, have more leisure time than younger people, and how they allocate this time. An extensive review of studies published before the mid-1960s concluded that most of them found that older people typically had about five hours more each day for leisure than young people.[49] Even though older people have more free time and can theoretically exercise more choice about how they spend this time, there are a number of constraints on their leisure. When a sample of older people was asked to identify some of them, the one most commonly mentioned was, curiously enough, a lack of time. Another major limitation, one considered in chapter 4, is declining health. Inadequate transportation and fear of crime also influence the leisure activities of older people.[50]

Changes in Leisure Activities over the Life Cycle

Leisure activities vary over the course of a person's life. The total number of activities declines with age, and the sorts of leisure pursuits also change. A major study, conducted in Houston in 1969 and 1970, found that there was a decline with age in activities requiring physical exertion: dancing, outdoor sports and recreation, travel, and hunting (for men). Several other less physically demanding activities also declined: reading and attending movies and cultural productions. Some others remained unchanged with age: television viewing, participation in discussions, attendance at spectator sports, membership in clubs and organizations, and entertaining guests.[51]

The findings of a cross-sectional analysis, such as this one, which is composed of individuals in several age groups must be interpreted with caution. Differences between age groups could be the result of factors other than age. They could, first, be due to educational differences between the generations since young people tend to be better educated than older people. Since the older population is composed of people in several different generations, what might appear to be age differences might, instead, be a reflection of changing life-styles over several generations.

Another study of life cycle changes asked people whether or not their leisure activities were different than they had been ten years before. It is hard to generalize the results of this study due to the methods used, since people estimated changes in their own activities in a retrospective manner. All of the respondents were members of a senior center and were an atypical group since they were highly educated (averaging 13.4 years of school), while almost half of them were women who had never married. Even though this study and the study done in Houston differed in their sample composition, the findings are quite similar. The senior center members spent less time in activities requiring physical exertion, more time as spectators, and about the same amount of time in solitary activities.[52]

Several other studies of leisure activities have found that older people spend more time in passive, solitary activities—mainly watching television and listening to the radio.[53] This increase is understandable since people tend to become more sedentary, have more time to fill, and also have fewer social ties.[54] Television can simultaneously fulfill several needs: it can provide companionship, transmit information, and be a way to structure time and to keep occupied. When people were asked to identify the reasons why they watched television, the most important need was for information. Relatively few people used television for "companionship" and most people who used television in this way were women or people who were living alone.[55]

Retirement and Leisure

Since retirement means that people spend less time working, then one consequence of retirement is an increase in the amount of available leisure time. The reverse might also be true: the desire to have more free time can also be a reason for retiring.[56] Even though retirement increases the objective amount of a person's free time, studies of the effects of retirement on leisure suggest that there is not a one-to-one correspondence in the reduction of work time and the perception of having more leisure, nor in the amount of time actually devoted to active leisure. A recent longitudinal study of respondents in a major survey, the Veteran's Administration's Normative Aging Study, found that retirees did not believe that they actually had more leisure time than they did when they were working.[57]

A very clear trend, supported by data in several large panel studies, is that the amount of time people spend in solitary and passive leisure pursuits increases when they retire.[58] Retirement does not appear to lead to significant changes in people's sense of the actual amount of time they have nor in the amount of time they actually devote to active leisure.

Informal Social Relationships of Older People

Involvement in informal social relationships—with friends, relatives, and neighbors—serves a number of important functions in the lives of older people. First, it positively influences their mental health.[59] Second, social networks serve as significant sources of help and assistance which enable people to cope with the tasks of daily living.[60]

There are several other ways informal relationships change in old age. They will be discussed in greater detail in subsequent chapters, but will be mentioned briefly at this point. First, people spend more time with their relatives (see chapter 3). Second, increasing age and declining health independently and together modify a person's social network. There are also differences in the ways aging and retirement affect different sorts of people—men and women, blacks and whites. Finally, people in various educational, occupational, and income groups respond differently to the aging process.

One task of this book is to examine the association between volunteering and informal social relationships. Previous studies have found that there is a negative relationship between the two: older volunteers are less involved in informal social interaction than nonvolunteers.[61] This association is reconsidered here. It is important to note that the social skills used in voluntary associations are probably the same as those used to develop friendships and maintain kinship relationships.[62]

Participation in Voluntary Associations

A good deal is known about older people's involvement in voluntary associations. Membership in voluntary association tends to decline during old age. However this decrease is very much conditioned by retirement, widowhood, age, health, gender, socioeconomic status, race, and religion—findings that will be more carefully documented later in the book.

This book will look at the connection between volunteering and formal social participation. Two previous studies, based on relatively small samples, both found that a major difference between older volunteers and those not involved in volunteering was that the former were more involved in voluntary groups in general.

Some Unanswered Questions

A number of questions relevant to understanding older people's leisure patterns and levels of social participation are pertinent to understanding the place of volunteering in older people's lives. Some of them cannot be completely answered but will be used to focus the discussion. Are older people involved in a smaller range of activities than young people? Do people change the kinds of activities they are engaged in as they age? What are some of the effects of increasing age and declining health on social activities? How do health and age individually and jointly influence social participation and leisure? To what extent are changes in old age due to generational differences or to socioeconomic differences between age groups? What are some of the differences between older men and women? Blacks and whites? Catholics, Protestants, and Jews? Are higher levels of activity a cause or a consequence of life satisfaction?

In the course of preparing this book, it became clear that volunteering by older people is not an isolated event in people's lives. Instead, it is part of a pattern of higher social and leisure involvement on the part of some older people. The book is primarily an examination of the social characteristics and social circumstances associated with volunteering by older people. It is, at the same time, a study of patterns of social and leisure participation by older people. Therefore, some of the questions posed in the previous paragraph, questions dealing with activities far broader than volunteering, are closely linked to the subject of this book.

Notes

1. M. Upp, "A Look at the Economic Status of the Aged: Then and Now," *Social Security Bulletin,* Vol. 45, No. 3, p. 19.

2. U.S. Bureau of the Census, *Historical Statistics of the United States: Colonial Times to 1970* (Washington, D.C.: U.S. Government Printing Office, 1975), Series A-37. U.S. Bureau of the Census, *Statistical Abstracts of The United States 1986* (Washington, D.C.: U.S. Government Printing Office, 1985), table 29.

3. J.O. Siegel and C.M. Taeuber, "Demographic Perspectives on the Long-Lived Society," *Daedalus,* 1986, Vol. 115, No. 1, p. 77

4. B.L. Neugarten and D.A. Neugarten, "Age in the Aging Society," *Daedalus,* 1986, Vol. 115, No. 1, p. 33.

5. N.J. Osgood, "Work: Past, Present and Future," in N.J. Osgood, ed., *Life After Work* (New York: Praeger, 1982), p. 18.

6. *Statistical Abstracts of the United States 1986,* Table 606.

7. Louis Harris and Associates, Aging in the Eighties: America in Transition (Washington, D.C.: National Council on the Aging, 1982), p. 29. C. Ventura and E. Worthy, "Voluntary Action and Older Americans: A Synthesis of Significant Data" (Washington, D.C.: National Council on the Aging, 1982), p. 4.

8. Gallup Organization, *Americans Volunteer—1981* (Princeton, N.J.: Gallup Organization, 1981), p. 12. Ventura and Worthy, op. cit., p. 4.

9. C. Lambert, M. Guberman, and R. Morris, "Reopening Doors to Community Participation for Older People: How Realistic?" *Social Service Review,* 1964, Vol. 38, p. 42. See also G. Worthington, "Older Persons as Community Service Volunteers," *Social Work,* 1963, Vol. 8, No. 4, pp. 71–75.

10. G. Einstein, "The Retired Social Worker as a Volunteer," *Social Casework,* 1973, Vol. 54, No. 1, pp. 37–41.

11. "Post-Partum Support by Foster Grandparents of Young Mothers At-Risk of Child Maltreatment: A Joint Program of the New York City Department for the Aging and the Presbyterian Hospital in the City of New York" (New York: n.d.) See also D. Gentry, "Grandmothers Who Fight Abuse with LOVE," *Modern Maturity,* October-November 1982, pp. 44–47.

12. E.R. Levine, "Training Elderly Volunteers in Skills to Improve the Emotional Adjustment of Children in a Day Care Center," *Dissertation Abstracts International,* July 1982, Vol. 43, No. 1, #78003393.

13. S. Baggett, "Attitudinal Consequences of Older Adult Volunteers in the Public School Setting," *Educational Gerontology,* 1981, Vol. 7, pp. 21–31.

14. "Grandparents Go to Jail," *Modern Maturity,* June-July 1984, Vol. 27, No. 3, p. 104.

15. J. Piper, "Retirees Lend a Helping Hand at Foote Hospital, East," *Michigan Hospitals,* January 1978, pp. 20–21.

16. J. Sainer and F. Kallen, "SERVE: A Case Illustration of Older Volunteers in a Psychiatric Setting," *The Gerontologist,* Spring 1972, Vol. 12, No. 1, pp. 90–93.

17. M. Foster, "SCOREing in the Retirement Years," *Perspectives on Aging,* 1983, Vol. 12, No. 6, p. 25.

18. W. Sykes, "Retirees in the Peace Corps: New Careers with Respect," *Generations,* Summer 1981, Vol. 5, No. 4, pp. 32–34.

19. S. Friedman, "Resident Welcoming Committee: Institutionalized Elderly in Volunteer Services to Their Peers," *The Gerontologist,* 1975, Vol. 15, pp. 362–67. L.M. Harvey, "The Activist Self-Help Program: An Alternative Service for the Aged," *Activities, Adaptation and Aging,* 1983, Vol. 4, No. 1, pp. 1–10. D. Kozak and J. Degar, "Elderly Volunteers in the Service of the Elderly," *The Gerontologist,* 1982, Vol. 22, pp. 208–9.

20. A. Babic, "The Older Volunteer: Expectations and Satisfactions," *The Gerontologist,* 1972, Vol. 12, pp. 87–90. See also F.M. Carp, "Differences among Older Workers, Volunteers, and Persons Who Are Neither," *Journal of Gerontology,* 1968, Vol. 23, p. 497; and Einstein, op. cit., p. 37.

21. Harris, op. cit.

22. See Susan Maizel Chambré and Ida B. Lowe, "Volunteering by the Elderly: A Bibliography for Researchers and Practitioners," *Journal of Volunteer Administration,* 1984, Vol. 2, No. 2, pp. 35–44.

23. J. Sainer and M. Zander, *SERVE: Older Volunteers in Community Service* (New York: Community Service Society, 1971), p. 205.

24. Ibid., p. 172.

25. S.M. Chambré, "Is Volunteering A Substitute for Role Loss in Old Age: An Empirical Test of Activity Theory," *The Gerontologist,* 1984, Vol. 24, No. 3, pp. 294–95.

26. Lambert et al., op. cit., p. 48.

27. Ventura and Worthy, op. cit., p. 13.

28. Chambré, op. cit., p. 295.

29. Lambert et al., op. cit. A. Monk and A. Cryns, "Predictors of Voluntaristic Intent among the Aged," *The Gerontologist,* 1974, Vol. 14, pp. 425–29. See also A. Rosenblatt, "Interest of Older Persons in Volunteer Activities," *Social Work,* Vol. 11, No. 3, pp. 87–91.

30. ACTION, *Americans Volunteer—1974: A Statistical Study of Volunteers in the United States* (Washington, D.C.: ACTION, 1975).

31. D. Dye, M. Goodman, M. Roth, N. Bley, and K. Jensen, "The Older Adult Volunteer Compared to the Non-Volunteer," *The Gerontologist,* 1973, Vol. 13, No. 3, pp. 215–18. See also K.I. Hunter and M.W. Linn, "Psychosocial Differences between Elderly Volunteers and Non-Volunteers," *International Journal of Aging and Human Development,* 1980–81, Vol. 12, No. 3, pp. 205–13. See also J. Mellinger and R. Holt, "Characteristics of Elderly Participants in Three Types of Leisure Groups," *Psychological Reports,* 1982, Vol. 50, No. 2, pp. 447–58.

32. Chambré, op. cit., pp. 294–95; Harris, op. cit., 1981, p. 30; Lambert et al., op. cit., p. 48.

33. Carp, op. cit., p. 500.

34. Dye et al., p. 217.

35. Mellinger and Holt, op. cit., p. 456.

36. L.C. Michelon, "The New Leisure Class," *American Journal of Sociology,* 1954, Vol. 59, pp. 371–78.

37. C. Buhler, "Meaningful Living in the Mature Years," in R.W. Kleemeier, ed., *Aging and Leisure* (New York: Oxford, 1961), pp. 345–46. F. Itzin, "Social Relations," in A.M. Hoffman, ed., *The Daily Needs and Interests of Older People* (Springfield, Ill.: C.C. Thomas, 1970), pp. 141–46.

38. Z.S. Blau, *Old Age in a Changing Society* (New York: F. Watts, 1973), pp. 22–36. See also I. Rosow, "The Social Context of the Aging Self," *The Gerontologist,* 1973, Vol. 3, No. 1, pp. 82–84.

39. R.J. Havighurst, B.L. Neugarten, and S.S. Tobin, "Disengagement and Patterns of Aging," in B.L. Neugarten, ed., *Middle Age and Aging* (Chicago: University of Chicago Press, 1968), p. 161.

40. A. Roadberg, "Perceptions of Work and Leisure among the Elderly," *The Gerontologist,* 1981, Vol. 21, No. 2, pp. 142–45.

41. C. Buhler, "Meaningful Living in the Mature Years," in R.W. Kleemeier, ed., op. cit., pp. 349–51.

42. R.J. Havighurst, "Leisure and Aging," in A.M. Hoffman, ed., op. cit., p. 165.

43. P.M. Lawton, "Leisure Activities for the Aged," *The Annals of the American Academy of Political and Social Science,* June 1978, Vol. 438, p. 75.

44. *Historical Statistics,* Series D-35, p. 132. *Statistical Abstracts,* 1985, Table 660.

45. B.D. Karl, "Lo the Poor Volunteer: An Essay on the Relation between History and Myth," *Social Service Review,* 1984, Vol. 58, pp. 497–98.

46. R. Atchley, "The Leisure of the Elderly," *The Humanist,* September/October 1977, pp. 14–16.

47. R.C. Atchley, "Retirement and Leisure Participation: Continuity or Crisis," *The Gerontologist,* Spring 1971, Vol. 11, Part I, pp. 13–17. See also S.J. Miller, "The Social Dilemma of the Aging Leisure Participant," in A. Rose and W. Peterson, eds., *Older People and their Social World* (Philadelphia: F.A. Davis, 1965), p. 84.

48. Atchley, "Retirement and Leisure Participation: Continuity or Crisis," op. cit., p. 16.

49. M.W. Riley and A. Foner, *Aging and Society, Volume I: An Inventory of Research Findings* (New York: Russell Sage Foundation, 1968), p. 513.

50. F.A. McGuire, "Constraints on Leisure Involvement in the Later Years," in P.M. Foster, ed., *Activities and the "Well Elderly"* (New York: Haworth Press, 1983).

51. C. Gordon, C.M. Gaitz, and J. Scott, "Leisure and Lives: Personal Expressivity across the Life Span," in R. Binstock and E. Shanas, eds., *Handbook of Aging and the Social Sciences* (New York: Van Nostrand Reinhold, 1976), pp. 327–28.

52. M. Zborowski, "Aging and Recreation," *Journal of Gerontology,* 1962, Vol. 17, No. 3, pp. 302–9.

53. J. Hoar, "A Study of Free-time Activities of 200 Aged Persons," *Sociology and Social Research,* 1961, Vol. 45, No. 2, pp. 157–63. See also E.P. Nystrom, "Activity Patterns and Leisure Concepts among the Elderly," *The American Journal of Occupational Therapy,* 1974, Vol. 28, No. 6, pp. 337–45.

54. R. Meyersohn, "A Critical Examination of Commerical Entertainment," in R.W. Kleemeier, ed., op. cit., p. 264.

55. A.M. Rubin and P.B. Rubin, "Older Persons' T.V. Viewing Patterns and Motivations," *Communication Research,* 1982, Vol. 9, No. 2, pp. 287–313.

56. R.J. Havighurst, "The Future Aged: The Use of Time and Money," *The Gerontologist,* 1975, Vol. 15, Supplement, p. 14.

57. R. Bossé and D.J. Ekerdt, "Change in Self-Perception of Leisure Activities with Retirement," *The Gerontologist,* 1981, Vol. 21, No. 6, p. 651.

58. E. Palmore, *Social Patterns in Normal Aging: Findings from the Duke Longitudinal Studies* (Durham, N.C.: Duke University Press, 1981), p. 43. See also A. Foner

and K. Schwab, *Aging and Retirement* (Monterey, Calif: Brooks/Cole, 1981), pp. 40–41; and Bossé and Ekert, op. cit., p. 651.

59. M.F. Lowenthal, "Social Isolation and Mental Illness in Old Age," *American Sociological Review,* 1964, Vol. 29, No. 1, pp. 54–70.

60. M.H. Cantor, "The Informal Support System: Its Relevance in the Lives of the Elderly," in E. Borgatta and N. McClusky, eds., *Aging and Society* (Beverly Hills, Calif.: Sage, 1980), pp. 131–44.

61. Dye et al., op. cit., Mellinger and Holt, op. cit.

62. D.E. Giles and C.E. Young, "Participation in Voluntary Associations and Informal Helping Networks: A Study of Two Forms of Community Interaction," paper presented at the 1984 Conference of the Association of Voluntary Action Scholars, November 4, 1984, Boston, Mass.

2
Study Population and Research Methods

This book looks at a broad range of possible correlates of volunteering in the older population. It considers a series of social characteristics that might distinguish between older people who are involved in doing volunteer work and people who do not participate in such activities. Chapters 3 through 8 look at a number of individual characteristics that might be related to volunteering; these include indicators of role loss, demographic and socioeconomic characteristics, as well as patterns of involvement in other types of leisure activities. The book builds on earlier research in two ways. It looks at the associations between volunteering and independent variables examined in earlier research: role loss, demographic, and socioeconomic characteristics. However, it makes some finer distinctions both within and between groups. For example, many studies compare retirees with people who are still working. This book also looks at people who never retired but are working on a part-time basis, and those who are semiretired.

A second general area of interest is the interrelationship between volunteering, involvement in other sorts of social and leisure activities, and a person's level of life satisfaction. This portion of the book addresses a central issue in the field of social gerontology—whether or not older people's well-being is improved by their being more involved in a variety of social and leisure activities. This is an especially appropriate issue for this book since a major reason for promoting volunteering by the elderly is to improve the quality of their lives. Several excellent studies do look at the possible effects of volunteering on life satisfaction. However, the conclusions they reach should be viewed cautiously since most of them use relatively small samples composed of people who live in one geographic area or who participate in one program for older volunteers. Since the present book includes a large and representative sample, its findings on the associations between volunteering, leisure, and life satisfaction should augment existing studies on this subject.

Description of the Sample

The analysis is based on data drawn from a 1981 survey sponsored by the National Council on Aging (NCOA). Louis Harris and Associates conducted the interviews and wrote an extensive report entitled *Aging in the Eighties: America in Transition.*[1] A similar study was also sponsored by NCOA in 1974.[2]

The survey involved interviews with 3,427 adults. A disproportionate number of them were 55 and over (n = 2,359) in order to make sure that there were a sizeable number of elderly respondents and people who were within a decade of reaching the traditional lower limit of being considered elderly.

Social researchers have used the age of 65 as a lower limit for being included in studies of older people. This age was selected because it has been the traditional retirement age and because it was used to determine eligibility for old age pensions in a number of societies, including the United States. A wider age range is used for this book, which looks at people who were over the age of 60 in 1981 (n = 2,088). There are several reasons why this was done. Even though 65 is probably still viewed as the point of crossing into old age by most people, it is actually a less meaningful demarcation point between middle age and old age than it may have been in the past.[3] A large number of Americans are retiring before 65 and are choosing to have reduced Social Security benefits at 62 rather than full benefits at 65. Private pensions are also now more available to early retirees. In fact, retirement at 62 is becoming more common than retirement at 65. A large proportion of the people in this sample who were between 60 and 64 were fully retired (40 percent) and only one third in this age group were working on a full-time basis.

Although it is still important for symbolic reasons—most people probably still think of it as the age when a person becomes "elderly"—the age of 65 is also less meaningful because some older people at the other end of the age range now remain in the labor force well past the age of 65. The gradual elimination of mandatory retirement will probably prolong some people's worklives. Even today, almost one in eight people between 70 and 79 in this sample continued to work.

Respondents between the ages of 60 and 64 were also included in the analysis because some programs for older volunteers do not necessarily use reaching age 65 as criteria for participation. Some, such as RSVP, include all people who are retired regardless of their ages. Others use ages lower than 65 as a cutoff for entry.

Variables in the Analysis

Volunteering

Volunteering has been defined in several ways by social researchers. The major distinction is between formal and informal participation. Some studies concentrate on volunteering that occurs within the context of a formal organization. This procedure was used in two studies conducted by the U.S. Bureau of the Census in 1965 and 1974.[4] The interviews included a question in which respondents were asked if they ever did volunteer work for an organization and were given a list of types of organizations (for example, Scouts, civic associations, hospitals, and educational institutions). A second way to distinguish between volunteers and nonvolunteers is to ask people directly, without providing any additional information that might limit the number of volunteers identified. This has the advantage of not excluding people who might have worked for organizations that were inadvertently excluded from the list of possible contexts in which to be a volunteer. This approach was used for this analysis. The respondents were asked, "Apart from any work you're paid for, do you do any volunteer work or not?" The total sample consists of 480 people who did volunteer and 1,608 nonvolunteers.

Several other surveys sponsored by Independent Sector and conducted by the Gallup Organization in 1981 and 1983 used yet a third approach. They identified volunteers as "working in some way to help others for no monetary pay" and identified several possible examples of good deeds that are not usually considered to be volunteering. For example, helping neighbors by assisting them in various household chores (such as repairing items and moving) were identified as two types of volunteer activities.

The precise wording significantly influences the proportion of people who are then classified as volunteers. When informal assistance to neighbors and friends are included in volunteering, as was done in the two Gallup surveys, a substantially higher proportion of people were then defined as volunteers. Slightly less than one-quarter of respondents who were 65 or older who were interviewed for the 1981 Harris survey (which is used in this book) defined themselves as volunteers[5] as compared to 37 percent in the Gallup survey done in the same year.[6]

The pattern of responses suggests that when people are asked to provide their own definition of volunteering, they probably view it as unpaid work and do not include informal activities. This conclusion is based on the fact that the proportion of older volunteers in the Harris survey is much closer to those in the two government surveys (one of which was done in the same year, 1974) than those in the two studies conducted under the auspices of Independent Sector.

Independent Variables

One study or another has explored most of the independent variables that might be associated with patterns of volunteering by older people. This discussion provides a brief overview of the topics to be considered in this book. Individual chapters have their own literature reviews.

Role Loss. A rigorous investigation of the effects of role loss requires a longitudinal study in which people are asked the same or similar questions at two or more points in time so changes in attitudes or behavior can be measured. This book, by virtue of the fact that it is cross-sectional since respondents were only interviewed once, cannot accurately assess the effects of role loss. The measures of role loss are marital status, employment status, one measure of family involvement (frequency of providing assistance to family members), and a measure of what retirees missed about work (work deprivation). Since most discussions of older volunteers view role loss as a major motivation, this issue is considered in chapter 3 before other possible correlates of volunteering.

Age and Perceived Health. Increasing age and declining health are two major changes experienced by older people. The impact of each of these on volunteering is considered in chapter 4. Even though the two are intertwined, they do, in fact, have different meanings. Changes in health might influence a person's ability to volunteer. Apart from changes in health associated with increasing age, the nature and number of a person's social relationships also change with age. The individual effects and also the combined effects of each of these factors are examined in chapter 4.

Socioeconomic Indicators. The older population is a diverse one in terms of educational level, current or former occupation, and income. These characteristics are associated with social participation and leisure activities at all age levels. People with different occupational skills and educational levels also differ in what they bring to a job as a volunteer. The importance of these variables is considered in chapter 5.

Demographic Characteristics. Gender, race, and religion are all ascribed status characteristics influencing social participation, leisure, and volunteering. Women have traditionally been a major source of volunteers, especially women who are homemakers. Chapter 6 looks at some of the effects of gender on older people's volunteer participation. It explores some of the differences between older men and older women, and between older women who are working, those who are retired, and homemakers.

Recent changes in women's work patterns are affecting the composition of the older population. An increasing number of older women are retirees and, conversely, a declining proportion of them have spent most of their lives as homemakers. In this respect, older women are becoming a more diverse group. It is worthwhile to examine patterns of volunteering within and between gender categories in order to consider if there are significant differences within the older population that result from changing sex roles. The book looks at women with different employment histories as well as men and women in similar employment categories and occupations.

Racial and religious differences in the older population have been the object of some study, but information on the relationship between these characteristics and volunteering is limited. These variables are considered in chapter 7.

Social Participation and Leisure. Volunteering occurs within the context of other types of social and leisure pursuits. The connection between volunteering and other sorts of free-time activities has merited some attention, but the strength and nature of the relationships are still understood very little. Chapter 8 looks at the association between volunteering and a series of indicators in great detail.

Life Satisfaction. Social gerontologists have paid considerable attention to the subject of the level of well-being of older people; volunteering has been proposed as an important way to improve their life satisfaction. The interview included a widely used index of life satisfaction (the LSI-A index) an eighteen-item index originally developed by Neugarten and subsequently modified by Adams.[7] The association between volunteering and life satisfaction is discussed in chapter 9. This discussion also addresses a broader issue—whether people with high levels of social participation are a self-selected group.

Methods of Analyzing Data

Several statistical tools and methods of analyzing data are used. Most of the discussion draws upon cross-tabulations used to identify whether or not two variables are associated with each other. In many instances, three variables are used, one of which serves as a control in order to determine whether the association between volunteering and another factor is a "real" one or whether it is due to another reason. For example, people who are widowed volunteer less frequently than people who are still married. Widows and widowers are also generally older than married people. Age is introduced as a third, or control, variable in order to look at whether there is a real association between being widowed and volunteering or whether this association is due to age differences between the widowed and the married. Some portions of the analysis use two other statistical methods, analysis of variance and correlation, in order to establish the existence and, in the case of correlation, the strength of relationships.

One of the goals of the book is to investigate the interrelationships among all of the variables influencing volunteer participation within the older population. The statistical method used in this portion of the book is called path analysis. This relatively new method is useful in policy-oriented research since the models that can be developed provide information on the direct and indirect influences of a number of variables on a dependent variable. They also include information on the interrelationships among the factors that have an effect on the dependent variable. Chapter 10 uses this method and discusses how all of the variables previously found to influence volunteering are related to each other and, in the context of other factors, how they affect volunteering. This model serves as a reference point for the book's implications and policy recommendations constituting the final chapter, chapter 11.

Notes

1. Harris, op. cit.
2. L. Harris and Associates, *The Myth and Reality of Aging in America* (Washington, D.C.: National Council on the Aging, 1974).
3. For a discussion of this, see Neugarten, op. cit., 1986, pp. 33–34.
4. ACTION, op. cit.; and U.S. Department of Labor, *Americans Volunteer,* Manpower/Automation Research Monograph No. 10 (Washington, D.C.: U.S. Government Printing Office, 1969).
5. Harris, op. cit., 1981, p. 30.
6. Gallup, op. cit., p. 3.
7. B.L. Neugarten, R.J. Havighurst, and S. Tobin, "The Measurement of Life Satisfaction," *Journal of Gerontology,* 1961, Vol. 16, pp. 134–43. D. Adams, "Analysis of a Life Satisfaction Index," *Journal of Gerontology,* 1969, Vol. 24, pp. 470–74.

3
Volunteering as a Role Substitute: Widowhood, Retirement, and Volunteering

The way people allocate their time is structured by the demands of various social roles during most of their lives. Work and family responsibilities are especially important during adulthood, and their impact varies over the life cycle. The demands of working can vary in intensity. Family obligations are also affected by a number of things, among them changes in the ages of a person's children as well as shifts in the emotional needs of a spouse, of parents, and of siblings.

The most significant changes in a person's roles during old age are the result of retirement and widowhood. The impact of these two events on the course of people's lives led to a common view among gerontologists that old age is a period of role loss and that the older person's life is roleless.[1]

Activity theory, a major perspective in social gerontology, suggests that people adapt better to the aging process when they engage in role substitution.[2] This process is beneficial for several reasons. It allows a person to maintain a stable level of social involvement at a time when various commitments are being reduced. By acquiring new roles, a person can receive the same gratification from them as was previously obtained from the lost roles. For example, a person who received a great deal of satisfaction from being a parent can gain fulfillment by becoming a foster grandparent. Role substitution could also enhance an older person's life because the new roles are not substitutes as much as strategies for accommodating to the aging process. New roles can offer a different sort of emotional gratification and positively affect a person's level of well-being even though they might be quite different from earlier roles.

These perspectives have had an important impact on how social workers and volunteer administrators view older volunteers. They have also influenced discussions of the role volunteering plays in the lives of older people. Volunteering is primarily described as a way older people can successfully adapt to old age in the face of the loss of work and family roles. It is seen to be one way to fill the gaps in people's lives which can be created by retirement and by widowhood.[3]

As a work substitute, volunteering provides a number of things: a place to go on a particular day at a specified time,[4] a reason to get dressed (and dressed up) in the morning, and a context in which to develop and maintain friendships. It can also compensate for the reduction of family responsibilities by providing a person with the social ties and emotional gratification of family relationships. This view of volunteering is summarized in the following passage:

> For the older person who has perhaps suffered a loss—retirement from work, loss of peer relationships, death of parents and/or spouse, departure of grown children, or loss of feelings of self-worth and dignity—the opportunity to share and to give service is poignantly valuable. To be able to continue to contribute when one has been reduced to accepting services—an uncomfortable role for many—is most satisfying. Returning to the nurturing role: sharing one's skills and life experience, and having a destination for which one must dress and leave one's house, can provide the raison d'etre for an older adult.[5]

Since the view that volunteering is a role substitute for older people is implicit in many discussions of older volunteers and has shaped programs intended to increase their participation, the first correlates examined in this book were indicators of role loss.

Review of the Literature

A great deal has been written about the family relationships of older people. Most of it has centered on the consequences of becoming widowed. The loss of a spouse is, indeed, a major event in a person's life and can have a significant impact on a number of areas of a person's experience.

The impact of widowhood is conditioned by a number of factors. There are substantial social class, gender, and racial differences in adjustment to widowhood.[6] Since children, grandchildren, and siblings are important sources of assistance and emotional support, involvement with other relatives can buffer the effects of widowhood. Interaction with relatives actually increases during old age.[7]

Another consequence of becoming widowed is beginning to live alone. Over the past few decades, the proportion of older people who live alone has increased dramatically, especially for women. In 1940, 10 percent of older men and older women were living alone.[8] In 1984, this had increased to 15 percent for men and was close to three times greater for women since 41 percent of older women were living alone.[9]

Retirement

Retirement is probably the most often studied aspect of the aging experience. It has become more common over the past century so that now it is almost universal. A shift toward early retirement is a more recent trend.

There is considerable variation in how people define retirement and what it means to them. For some, it is a form of liberation which frees them from work responsibilities. This freedom allows them to choose how to spend their time instead of having it structured for them by the demands of a job. For others, retirement is a signal of no longer being needed because of limited job skills, poor health, or merely being too old; this form of retirement has been called "abandonment." There are therefore two types of retirement;[10] for some people it reminds them that they have been pushed out of the work force, while for others, it is an opportunity to do a variety of things. Some people are pulled into retirement while others are pushed out of the work force.

The typical length of retirement has become significantly longer during the past several decades because people tend to both retire at younger ages and live longer. This poses a considerable challenge to social planners and to older people themselves: to transform the rolelessness of old age into a meaningful time of life.

Like widowhood, retirement is not a uniform experience. One source of variation is a person's occupation. Retirees differ greatly as to the kinds of jobs they retire from: the prestige, job satisfaction, and financial rewards vary. A second dimension is whether or not a person's retirement was voluntary or involuntary. This has a major influence on how a person adapts to retirement and his or her level of life satisfaction after retirement. Several research studies have reached the conclusion that people adjust better to retirement if it has been voluntary.[11]

Effects of Role Loss on Leisure: Empirical Findings

Retirement and reduced family responsibilities increase the amount of discretionary time available to older people. In theory, older people can exercise greater choice about how they then spend time. Even though retirement and widowhood are normal and socially acceptable status transitions, they reduce a person's responsibilities and remove obligations that used to structure their time. Retirement and widowhood also reduce a person's chances of conforming to the key social value of keeping busy. Adaptation to retirement is especially difficult for people who have spent their lives in a work-oriented society, who may have not have had a great deal of leisure time, and who have little experience in finding meaningful ways to spend the increased amount of spare time that accompanies retirement.

In spite of the fact that retirement increases the amount of time available to people, there is no consistent evidence that it leads to an increase in social participation or that retirees spend more time in active leisure pursuits. Two common beliefs have led to the assumption that retirees would devote more time to social participation and to active leisure: first, that time is a fixed commodity; and second, that work and leisure are mutually exclusive, so that less time spent working means that more time is available for leisure.[12] However, many leisure activities and areas of social involvement are in fact linked to work.[13] Some forms of voluntary association participation and volunteering actually improve a person's job situation either by having a positive impact on the nature of the job itself (as occurs with a union) or by enabling a person to improve his job situation by developing social contacts which will be beneficial in a job or in one's own business. Many organizations like Kiwanis bring people in similar occupations together while, at the same time, being involved in community betterment projects. A second way volunteering is linked to work is that people in some jobs are expected to volunteer or be involved in community projects. These activities could influence their job situation. For some college professors, tenure and promotion are mainly contingent on job-related activities but outside activities are also given weight in these decisions.

Changes in work obligations might therefore change the incentives to participate in community activities. The reasons for participation might no longer be present once retired. This would also be true when a person retires involuntarily and views retirement as a form of abandonment. For such a person, continued involvement in a work-linked activity could reinforce a sense of embarrassment at being pushed out of the labor force.

Some recent research studies have pointed out that retirement does not lead to an expansion of social involvement. Data from the Duke Longitudinal Study are particularly useful inasmuch as the men who were interviewed were asked about how they spent their time before and after retirement. The typical retiree estimated that after retirement he worked 35 hours less each week. Retirees did spend more time in active leisure, about 7 hours each week. However, the amount of time devoted to sedentary or solitary activities increased much more—to an average of 45 hours each week.[14] This study suggests, then, that when men retire, they allocate significantly more time to activities that are essentially passive and do not bring them into contact with other people.

There is some empirical support for the adequacy of another theoretical perspective on old age, continuity theory. According to this view, older people tend to continue to engage in the same forms of activity over the life cycle.[15] A recent study, which analyzed data from the Social Security Administration's Retirement History Survey, shows significant continuity in leisure. Respondents were asked to compare the amount of time devoted to a series of activities at two points in time, in 1971 and in 1975. These included watching television, going to restaurants, doing volunteer work, going to club meetings, and attending church. The study found a substantial amount of stability for both workers and retirees; both spent fairly similar amounts of time in these pursuits.[16]

Retirement has been treated as a dependent variable and as an independent variable. When it has been used as a dependent variable, researchers have considered a variety of factors that influence retirement, such as mandatory retirement policies and measures of a person's ability to work. When used as an independent variable, the focus has been on the possible effect of retirement on health status or on various measures of wellbeing. Havighurst points out that it is important to think about the interrelationship between leisure and retirement in another way: while retirement affects the amount of available leisure time, in addition, a desire to expand leisure is a reason why people retire.

> As the economic welfare of elderly people improves, more and more persons become able to choose when to retire. Retirement becomes a commodity to be purchased. A person who values leisure, or who has a variety of interesting demands on his time, will purchase retirement if he has enough savings and enough guaranteed pension income. His decision to retire will depend on his interest in his work; his desire for more leisure; his probable retirement income; the demand of the labor market for his labor; the interests of other family members in work and leisure.[17]

The idea that role loss is an impetus to volunteering is central to many discussions. This view was first articulated in a profile of participants in one of the first programs for older volunteers, the SERVE program. A substantial proportion of the participants were relatively uninvolved in work and family roles: two-thirds of them were not married and more than nine in ten were not working. These characteristics, as well as the fact that over half of the people originally joined the program in order to enhance their social contacts, led to the conclusion that volunteering was a response to role loss.[18]

Aside from this study, the view that role loss actually increases the tendency to volunteer has not received substantial support. Retirement has not been found to be a correlate of volunteering when researchers have looked at interest in doing volunteer work or actual participation.[19] Likewise, a person's marital status and the kind of household he or she lives in are also unrelated to participation.[20] Measures of role loss explained very little of the variance in volunteer participation in a study using data from the 1974 survey sponsored by ACTION.

Some Methodological Considerations in Studying Role Loss

Role loss refers to a process as well as to an end result; that is, it is a series of events in which the person's involvement in a social status changes. Role loss also means that a person becomes identified differently as a widow or as a retiree and then develops a different self-concept based on this new label. Since role loss involves a transition from one status to another, the most accurate way to pinpoint the effects of role loss is to use a panel study. This type of research design involves interviews or questionnaires done at two or more points in time; it allows a researcher to measure how a change at one point in time affects behavior or attitudes at a later time.

Since there is currently no large panel study that includes volunteering as a variable, studies based on existing data can only present tentative conclusions since they study behavior at only one point in time. They do not provide any information on whether or not behavior is the same as it was before widowhood or retirement. A valid study of the effects of role loss on volunteering would use a sample of people who were studied over time; it could then compare involvement in volunteering before and after retirement or widowhood. This book is therefore not able to really look at the effects of role loss on volunteering. What it does, instead, is consider the association between indicators of current involvement in work and family roles and whether or not a person is involved in doing volunteer work.

Studies of retirement have commonly divided older people into two categories, those who are working and those who have retired. A wider range of categories can be considered here: people working full-time or part-time, retirees who are either fully or semiretired, and homemakers. It will become clear later on in this chapter that these are meaningful distinctions which have a substantial impact on this one area of social participation.

Measures of loss of family roles involve questions about marital status, living arrangements, and how much time was spent caring for other family members. Since our concern was involvement in family roles, individuals living with another person who defined themselves as a couple but who were not actually "married" were included in the married category. A question concerning the amount of time spent visiting relatives and friends was not included since it combined both friends and relatives together. Unfortunately, there was no information concerning relationships with siblings and children nor any retrospective data on the meaning of marriage and the impact of widowhood. Nonetheless, the interview data do provide some sense of the family lives of the respondents but not a very complete portrait.

Family Involvement and Volunteering

Several significant differences would appear within the study population if volunteering is a substitute for role loss. A larger proportion of widowed people would be volunteers than people who were still married. Widows, who had lost the marital role, would more often be involved than people who had never married. Other indicators of limited involvement in family life, such as living alone or spending relatively little time assisting relatives, would also be associated with a tendency to be involved in volunteering.

None of these expectations were confirmed in the data analysis. About one in four married people (26 percent) were volunteers compared to one in five who were widowed (19 percent). Widows were also less often involved than the formerly married (25 percent). These differences were statistically significant ($x^2 = 15.0$, $df = 3$, $p > .001$). Similarly, people living alone were less likely to be volunteers (21 percent) than those living with a spouse (26 percent). There was also an inverse relationship between participation and the amount of time spent with family members; volunteers were more often those who spent a lot (27 percent) or some (29 percent) time with family members rather than reporting hardly any (19 percent) such contact ($x^2 = 25.1$, $df = 2$, $p < .001$).

Since all forms of social participation decline with age, it is possible that the association between volunteering and marital status might be suppressed because of the fact that widows and those living alone tend, on average, to be older than people who are still married. The married people in the sample were close to 70 whereas the widowed were about four years older. Volunteering does not appear to be a substitute for the loss of family roles even when age differences are considered. In three of the four age categories, widows or widowers were significantly less often involved in volunteering than people who are still married. For example, in the 70-to-79 age group, one-quarter of married people and one-fifth of widows were involved in volunteering.

There is no indication, then, that volunteering tends to be a substitute for family involvement among the elderly. This does not mean, however, that it does not serve this purpose for some older people. One way to interpret these findings is to view the functions served by family involvement, the role played by volunteering, and the kinds of contexts in which they take place. Family involvement is not goal-oriented and mainly provides people with emotional support. Families are primary groups in which social interaction is rather intimate and is not guided by formal rules. Even though volunteer work can provide significant emotional gratification, it occurs within the context of a formal organization with specific rules and rather specific goals. Volunteering is therefore not an equivalent activity to family involvement, and it appears to be neither a substitute nor a way to compensate for reduced involvement in family life.

Volunteering as a Work Substitute

Since volunteering can be viewed as unpaid work, it is quite logical to assume that people are more often involved as volunteers if they are retired than if they continue to work. Even continuing to work on a part-time basis would limit the likelihood of volunteering.

As was the case with the measures of family involvement, there is also no evidence that a reduction in work activity is related to an increased tendency to volunteer. In fact, older people working on a full-time or a part-time basis are more often involved in volunteering (27 percent) than people who are fully retired (22 percent). The highest level of participation (34 percent) occurs for the semiretired, those who have retired but continue to work on a part-time basis. Thus, abandoning the work role totally appears to result in lower levels of participation whereas partial retirement is associated with significantly greater involvement.

A rather surprising finding, in view of some conclusions of earlier studies of volunteers and prevailing stereotypes concerning the role of homemakers as volunteers (an issue more extensively discussed in chapter 6), is that homemakers are the least often involved in doing volunteer work (18 percent) of any of the other categories. These findings are highly significant ($x^2 = 15.5$, $df = 4$, $p > .001$). One reason why people who continue to work are more often involved in volunteering than retirees is because retirees are, on the whole, older than people who are still working. (See table 3–1.) For almost the entire sample, the exception being the 80 and over category, there is fairly equal participation by people who are still working and those who are fully retired. There is a substantially higher level of participation by the semiretired in all of the age categories. The only instance where retirement seems to be associated with an increased tendency to be involved in volunteering is when people are retired but continue to work on a part-time basis.

These findings are consistent with an earlier study drawing upon data from the 1974 survey sponsored by ACTION. There, retirement was not associated with a higher tendency to volunteer even when age differences were considered.[22] However, the form of the questions did not permit a distinction to be made between partial and total retirement. Our understanding of why

Table 3–1
Percentage of Respondents Who Volunteer by Employment Status, Controlling for Age
(n = 2,046)

	Employment Status				Significance		
Age	Employed	Semiretired	Fully Retired	Homemaker	x^2	df	p
60 to 64	31 (105)	67 (9)	29 (96)	39 (36)	6.1	3	.10
65 to 69	26 (76)	34 (67)	27 (451)	15 (66)	6.5	3	>.05
70 to 79	23 (40)	29 (51)	22 (629)	17 (109)	3.0	3	n.s.
80 and over	0 (5)	25 (8)	11 (237)	12 (61)	2.3	3	n.s.

Note: Numbers in parentheses indicate number out of total sample who fall in that age and employment status category.
n.s. = not significant.

retirement is not generally associated with volunteering is greatly enhanced by the fact that the Harris survey included a broad range of questions concerning the circumstances under which the person retired. We now look at some of these questions in order to provide some reasons why volunteering is not a work-substitute.

Retirement Experiences of Volunteers and Nonvolunteers

There is a great range in the experiences of retirees. People adjust better to retirement when it occurs on a voluntary basis and is preceded by planning and preparation.[23] For people who retire voluntarily, increased leisure is not a problem they face but might be a major reason why they have retired. People who retired voluntarily are more likely to be involved in volunteering (26 percent) than those who stated that their retirement was not voluntary (20 percent). Volunteers also retired about one year earlier than nonvolunteers: the volunteers were 61.3 years old when they retired as compared to the nonvolunteers, whose average retirement age was 62.6, a difference that is statistically significant $(F = 8.2, p > .001)$.

Work Deprivation and Volunteering

Volunteering has many of the same features as working: it often occurs within a formal organization and is goal-oriented. It could therefore fulfill some of the gratifying aspects of working. The analysis included a series of seven items designed to tap work deprivation. Respondents were asked whether they missed the following aspects of working: contact with other people, the feeling of being useful, the respect that is gained, the fact that "things are happening," the work itself, the fixed schedule, and the income. These items were analyzed individually and were combined into an overall index of work deprivation which simply involved adding up all of the scores on the individual items.

The results are surprising. The volunteers actually miss work *less* than the nonvolunteers. This is true when the individual measures are considered as well as the overall scores. People who miss the structure imposed by work, the interpersonal relationships emerging in a work setting, the feeling of being useful, and the respect derived from working actually volunteered less often than people who indicated that they did not miss these things. The nonvolunteers also scored significantly higher $(\bar{x} = 4.3)$ on the overall measure of work deprivation than the nonvolunteers. $(\bar{x} = 3.6, F = 19.1, p < .001)$.

This was initially a puzzling finding. A closer look at some other research, however, revealed another study on a somewhat different topic whose findings are consistent with this book's. Using a relatively small sample of men and women retirees, the authors looked at the association between work orientations and two measures of adjustment to retirement—activity level and life satisfaction. People with high work orientations were less active when they retired. Retirees with high work orientations who did not view their daily activities as being useful had especially low levels of life satisfaction when they were retired.[24]

These findings suggest that there is a need to closely examine two notions: (1) that a reduction in time spent working leads to more involvement in active leisure pursuits in retirement and (2) that people use leisure activities to either compensate or substitute for work when they retire. Indeed, research studies described in the first chapter indicate that these do not occur and that retirees probably spend more time in solitary and sedentary activities than in active leisure or social relationships.

Another strand of research whose findings merit discussion are studies of the reasons why people become volunteers. Many of the general discussions indicate that people might be motivated by a desire to acquire the gratification from unpaid work that they do not receive in their own jobs. Yet, when this assumption has been empirically tested, it has not been supported.[25] People tend to select leisure activities and volunteer jobs that are consistent with their paid jobs rather than ones that either are complementary or provide compensation for a lack of job satisfaction.

Volunteering is not a work-substitute in another very important way: it offers no payment. Many people believe that any work worth doing is work that should merit payment. This is a particularly significant barrier to participation in volunteering because volunteers often do the same work as paid workers and can work alongside paid workers.

Summary

Activity theory suggests that people who lack or who lose significant social roles, especially work and family roles, compensate for these losses by finding role substitutes. This has been a common assumption in discussions of reasons why older people volunteer, ways to expand their participation, and the kinds of procedures that are effective in reinforcing their involvement.

This chapter has considered whether volunteering serves this purpose in older people's lives by looking at the possible associations between volunteer participation and various indicators of involvement in work and family roles. The data in the book do not support this view and, in fact, suggest that the reverse may be true: stronger ties to work and family roles are associated with a greater tendency to be involved in volunteering.

People who had been widowed did not volunteer more often than married people even when the older ages of the widows were taken into account. Retirement was not associated with an increased tendency to volunteer. Even when age differences were taken into consideration, there was no indication that the fully retired were more often involved in volunteering than people who continued to work. The partly retired donated their time more frequently than did those who were completely retired.

There are also differences in the retirement patterns and attitudes of volunteers and nonvolunteers. The volunteers tended to retire voluntarily at earlier ages, and they had lower levels of work deprivation than the nonvolunteers. The prevailing view on the subject—that volunteering is a substitute for the loss of work and family roles in old age—is confirmed neither in this book nor in a previous study conducted by this author using a sample of people interviewed seven years earlier. Volunteering does not appear to compensate or to substitute for either the socioemotional functions of family life or the various types of rewards received from working.

In addition to widowhood and retirement, the most significant changes that occur in older people's lives are increasing age and declining health. The next chapter looks at the possible association between volunteering and these variables.

Notes

1. Blau, loc. cit.
2. R. Havighurst, B. Neugarten, and S.S. Tobin, op. cit.
3. See Babic, op. cit.; Einstein, op. cit.; and Hunter and Linn, op. cit.
4. Rosenblatt, op. cit.
5. E.L. Swartz, "The Older Adult: Creative Use of Leisure Time," *International Journal of Geriatric Psychiatry,* 1978, Vol. 11, No. 1, p. 87.
6. H.H. Hyman, *Of Time and Widowhood* (Durham, N.C.: Duke University Press, 1983). H. Lopata, *Widowhood in an American City* (Cambridge, Mass.: Schenkman, 1973), pp. 71–76, 268–70.
7. See E. Shanas, "The Family as a Social Support System in Old Age," *The Gerontologist,* 1979, Vol. 19, No. 2, pp. 169–74. See also V.G. Cicirelli, "Adult Children and Their Elderly Parents," in T.H. Brubaker, ed., *Family Relationships in Later Life* (Beverly Hills, Calif.: Sage, 1983).
8. F.E. Kobrin, "The Primary Individual and the Family: Changes in Living Arrangements in the United States since 1940," *Journal of Marriage and the Family,* 1976, Vol. 36, p. 22.
9. *Statistical Abstracts of the United States 1986,* Table 31.
10. M. Baum and R.C. Baum, *Growing Old: A Societal Perspective* (Englewood Cliffs, N.J.: Prentice-Hall, 1980), pp. 4–6.
11. D.C. Kimmel, K.F. Price, and J.W. Walker, "Retirement Choice and Retirement Satisfaction," *Journal of Gerontology,* 1978, Vol. 33, No. 4, pp. 575–85. P.O. Peretti and G. Wilson, "Voluntary and Involuntary Retirement of Aged Males and Their Effect on Emotional Satisfaction, Usefulness, Self-Image, Emotional Stability, and Interpersonal Relationships," *International Journal of Aging and Human Development,* Vol. 6, No. 2, pp. 131–38.

12. J.J. Spengler, "Some Economic and Related Determinants Affecting the Older Worker's Occupational Role," in I.H. Simpson and J.C. McKinney, eds., *Social Aspects of Aging* (Durham, N.C.: Duke University Press, 1961), pp. 29–33.

13. H. Wilensky, "Life Cycle, Work Situation and Participation in Formal Associations," in R.W. Kleemeier, ed., op. cit., pp. 232–33.

14. Palmore, op. cit., p. 43.

15. B.L. Neugarten, *Personality in Middle and Late Life: Empirical Studies* (New York: Atherton, 1964).

16. Foner and Schwab, op. cit., p. 40.

17. Havighurst, op. cit., p. 14.

18. Sainer and Zander, op. cit., pp. 172, 205.

19. See Chambré, op. cit., pp. 294–95; Lambert et al., op. cit., p. 48; Monk and Cryns, op. cit., pp. 425–29; and Ventura and Worthy, op. cit., p. 13

20. Chambré, op. cit., p. 295. Hunter and Linn, op. cit., p. 208.

21. Chambré, op. cit.

22. Ibid., p. 294.

23. Kimmel et al., op. cit. See also Peretti and Wilson, op. cit.

24. K. Hooker and D.G. Ventis, "Work Ethic, Daily Activities, and Retirement Satisfaction," *Journal of Gerontology,* 1984, Vol. 39, pp. 478–84.

25. L.E. Miller, "Understanding the Motivation of Volunteers: An Examination of Personality Differences and Characteristics of Volunteers' Paid Employment," paper presented at the Annual Meeting of the Asociation of Voluntary Action Scholars, Blacksburg, Va., September 1984.

4
Age, Health Status, and Volunteering

I ncreasing age and declining health are the most salient changes taking place during later life. Increasing age is associated with changes in work patterns and in social relationships. Declining health leaves a person with less energy to carry on the tasks of daily living and to be involved in social relationships. Although age and health status are, in reality, so closely intertwined as to be inseparable, they do have independent effects. It is important to trace the different effects of each of them before looking at how they might influence volunteering. There are several significant changes in a person's social network during old age. Widowhood becomes more and more common. People's involvement with their relatives changes as children, grandchildren, and siblings grow older. These significantly modify a person's responsibilities as a spouse, a parent, a grandparent, or a sibling. Friendship networks and the nature of friendships probably change as people become older and are widowed. Friends move, they die, or their health deteriorates, all of which also lead to changes in social interaction. Retirement results in fewer and fewer friendships that are work-related.

The expectation that a person should stop working probably increases as people grow older. At the same time, retirement could become increasingly attractive when people want to be relieved of their work responsibilities and be free of the structure imposed by working.

An extensive review of research on the various factors contributing to higher levels of well-being in the older population concluded that declining health is the most important concern of older people:

> The most frequently reported dread of older persons is that health problems or disability will interfere with their capacity for independent living. . . . Indeed, fear of illness-related dependency surpasses fear of death among older individuals. . . . Thus health is an important dimension of life quality and is a cherished resource for the majority of adults.[1]

Social gerontologists have looked at the individual effects of increasing age and declining health but the number of studies on these subjects is relatively small in view of the importance of these subjects. The major purpose of this chapter is to look at the associations between volunteering, age, and health; age and health are considered separately and then together. It also reexamines the negative association between total retirement and volunteering by looking at whether the lower participation of fully retired people is mainly due to the fact that they are in poorer health than people who are semiretired.

Review of the Literature

Effects of Increasing Age on Social Participation

There are significant changes in social participation throughout the life cycle. Most of the studies looking at voluntary association membership and volunteering conclude that the level of participation for adults is a U-shaped distribution; it increases during their twenties and thirties, reaches its highest level at about the age of 45, and then begins to decline.[2] These shifts can be attributed to the ways involvement in work and family roles can either serve as constraints on membership or motivate people to participate. During the years when people are actively engaged in childrearing, a good deal of social participation is related to the school and leisure activities of one's children. Involvement in parent-teacher associations, school boards, or scouting organizations are examples of these. Many occupations or professions have organizations linking people doing similar work, and these types of organizations provide opportunities to volunteer.

The motivations to participate in the kinds of voluntary associations that are linked to a person's work or family become greatly reduced in old age. These changes, along with declining health, are used to explain the reduction in social participation after the age of 45.

Studies of changes in patterns of social participation during old age have focused on two major issues: (1) whether the levels of social participation exhibit continuity with earlier stages in the life cycle and (2) if the overall level of participation remains relatively stable in later life. An extensive review of this literature, which concentrated on voluntary association membership, revealed that there were rather different conclusions.

There is support for the premise that voluntary association participation remains stable in later life and also for the opposite conclusion, that there is a significant decline in membership during old age.[3] When another dependent variable (a total measure of social participation) is used, some studies confirm that overall activity remains constant.[4] Respondents interviewed in a major longitudinal survey conducted at Duke University did decrease their social activity as they grew older.[5] Some interesting differences appeared when measures of different types of activities were separated from each other. When pre- and postretirement activities were compared, retired men spent less time in activities that fostered social interaction and devoted much more time to solitary leisure activities.[6]

These studies look at very broad trends over the course of the entire life cycle or examine the over-65 population as a whole. It is also valuable to look closely at the levels of involvement after the sixth decade of life on a year-by-year basis in order to pinpoint more accurately the age when participation begins to decline steadily. The one study that did this surveyed older men and women in four rural communities in New York State in the late 1940s. It reached the conclusion that participation in nonreligious organizations did not decline substantially until a relatively late age, after the age of eighty.[7]

Health and Social Participation

Even though it is logical to conclude that declining health is a major source of the reduction of older people's social activity, the existing data do not consistently indicate that this is in fact the case. One study found a strong correlation between a person's level of physical functioning and a total measure of social activity.[8] Another study found that poor health was associated with a reduction in involvement in church-sponsored activities, but that health was not associated with the amount of time people spent with their friends and peers.[9]

When older people are asked to identify some of the things that limit their leisure time, poor health is not identified as being especially important. McGuire asked 125 older people who lived in a midwestern city to indicate some of the reasons why they were not engaged in leisure activities. Only 29 percent of them mentioned poor health as one of the constraints on their leisure. The more important limitations were not enough time, a lack of money, work responsibilities, or having more important things to do.[10]

There are also inconclusive results on whether health influences volunteering. A study conducted in St. Louis found that people who belonged to a volunteer service club were healthier than a group of their contemporaries who were not volunteers but attended a senior center.[11] A second study came to some different conclusions. It compared three groups: members of a senior center, residents of a housing project for the elderly, and patients at a Veterans Administration clinic. Volunteers and nonvolunteers had similar scores on several objective measures of health status: number of surgical operations, ability to be self-sufficient in daily living, and the amount of pain that people had. However, there were some other areas of difference. The volunteers were healthier in some ways (they had had fewer days of recent hospitalization and took fewer medications than nonvolunteers) but were less healthy in one very important way—they had more hearing or visual problems than the nonvolunteers.[12]

The association between health and volunteering has also been considered from another perspective: the effect of poor health on whether or not a volunteer continues to be involved in such activities. There have been two studies of this issue. The first of them relied on three study populations, one in Kansas City and two in Atlanta. All three of the groups were studied over time; the amount of time varied between two years for the Atlanta group and four years for the Kansas City respondents.[13] A second study looked at older people who responded to a call for participants in a Retired Senior Volunteer Program (RSVP); they were surveyed at two points six months apart.[14] The studies reached the same conclusion—poor health was the most important reason why people stopped doing volunteer work.

A common limitation of many of these studies is that they tend to use subjective measures of health which rely on respondents to rate their own health (which is also true for this analysis) rather than using either objective self-ratings or scores assigned by health care professionals. Many articles and books, including this one, look at perceived health rather than health status measured objectively. Yet, self-defined ratings, such as the one used here, are actually quite accurate and have a close correspondence to scores assigned by physicians.[15]

Combined Effect of Age and Health on
Social Participation

Since none of the studies reviewed actually look at the combined effect of health and age on leisure, voluntary association membership, or volunteering, this book fills a gap in our understanding of the individual and joint effects of age and health on volunteer participation. Using a broad age group, it is possible to focus on the age when volunteer participation actually begins to decline and to consider the separate and joint effects of health and age.

Research Methods

Two independent variables are used here: age and perceived health. Age is treated in two ways. In some portions of the analysis, it is used as an interval level measure, and the effects of year-by-year age increases are considered. Four age groups were created and used in other parts of the discussion. These groups include people who are close to retirement and those who have retired at relatively young ages (respondents who are between the ages of 60 and 64), people who are at the traditional retirement age of 65 or within four years beyond it (the 65-to-69 age group), and two other categories based on a distinction first made by Neugarten, the "young-old" (those between 70 and 79) and the "old-old" (respondents who were 80 years old or over when they were interviewed).

The measure of perceived health is based on two questions. In the first, respondents were asked to provide an assessment of their overall health status. A different aspect of perceived health was tapped in the second question which asked respondents whether poor health was a problem for them. The two questions are not correlated with each other ($r = .004$). An index of perceived health was created by combining responses to the two items; the scores for the index ranged from 2 to 7, and the mean score was 4.87. The variable is treated as an interval measure in some portions of the analysis. In other parts, the scores were divided into three categories: poor, good, and excellent.

Findings

Effects of Increasing Age on Volunteering

The tendency to be involved in volunteer work declines with age. The Pearson correlation coefficient between the two is a statistically significant one ($p < .001$, $r = -.14$). Another way to describe this relationship is to calculate the proportion of volunteers in each of the four age groups. Among the youngest (those approaching retirement or who had retired early), about one-third were involved as volunteers. The proportion declined for the retirement age group (to 27 percent) and dropped to about one in five for the 70-to-79 age group (22 percent). The sharpest decline was for the 80-and-over group, only one in ten of whom were engaged in volunteering ($x^2 = 45.0$, $df = 2$, $p < .001$).

Figure 4–1 illustrates that even though the overall trend in volunteering declines, each age increment does not lead to a reduction in participation. After the age of 77, the downward trend is clearer. This is similar to a finding mentioned earlier, that participation in voluntary associations does not decline radically until after the age of 80.

It is also important to note that even though there is a substantial decline, the level of participation among the old-old is relatively high. One in ten of them is involved in doing volunteer work, and some of them have a paid job at the same time.

Effects of Perceived Health on Volunteering

Declining health is commonly assumed to be a major reason why older people reduce their involvement in a variety of social and leisure activities. Empirical studies have reached contradictory results: some support this observation, while others do not. The data included in this survey are appropriate for a reexamination of this question with respect to volunteering.

Like most older people, the people who were interviewed for this survey were relatively free of health problems. Slightly less than one-quarter indicated that poor health was a very serious problem. The most important health-related concern was a decline in energy level; close to half (46 percent) indicated that this was a very serious problem.

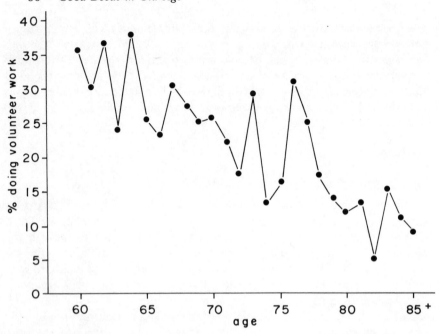

Figure 4–1. Percentage of Older People Doing Volunteer Work According to Age

There is, in fact, a strong relationship between volunteering and perceived health. People who define their health more favorably tend to be volunteers. It is also possible that the direction of this relationship is quite different, that volunteering improves people's perception of their health. This is a strong possibility since the interviews provide a subjective picture of health; none of the questions asked about specific physical impairments that could limit a person's ability to volunteer. The association between perceived health and volunteering is a significant one ($p < .001$) since the Pearson correlation coefficient between whether or not a person volunteered and the raw score on the health measure is $r = .21$. One-third of respondents who defined themselves as in excellent health were volunteers, as compared to one in five in good health, and one in ten in poor health ($x^2 = 86.7$, $df = 2$, $p < .001$).

Perceived health is more closely related to volunteering than is increasing age since the correlation between volunteering and perceived health is a stronger one ($r = -.21$) than is the relationship between age and volunteering ($r = -.14$).

Combined Effect of Age and Perceived Health
on Volunteering

One reason why there is an association between volunteering and age could be that people's health declines as they become older. To consider whether this is the case, perceived health was controlled, and the relationship between age and volunteering was recalculated. Age has a negative effect on volunteering which is independent of the fact that increasing age is accompanied by declining health. The association between volunteering and age is reduced only slightly and remains significant when perceived health is controlled ($r = -.12$, $p < .001$).

To illustrate this graphically, figure 4–2 shows the percentage of people who were volunteers at each age level, dividing the respondents into three groups according to their perception of their health status: poor, good, and excellent. The figure shows that people who are in poor health volunteer far less often than

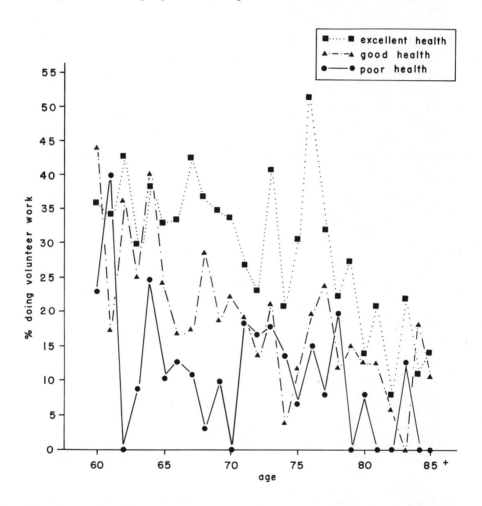

Figure 4–2. Percentage of Older People Doing Volunteer Work by Age According to Perceived Health

those in any of the other health categories and that this occurs irrespective of age. Those in excellent health are most often volunteers at every age. An important finding, one which is not evident in the calculation of a correlation coefficient but is illustrated more clearly in figure 4–2, is that perceived health becomes less important after the age of 77, the age when volunteering begins to decline consistently regardless of health. After the age of 77, the percentage of older volunteers declines for people in excellent health as well as for those in poor health.

Except for people approaching their eighties, age and perceived health each have an independent effect on volunteering. When age is controlled, the partial correlation coefficient between volunteering and perceived health is significant ($r = .20, p < .001$). As mentioned earlier, the association between volunteering and age continued to be significant when perceived health was controlled.

A different way to illustrate the independent effects of declining health and increasing age is to prepare a contingency table with all three variables (table 4–1). This table shows that the proportion of people who do volunteer work increases with more favorable health in all four age categories. For example, in the 80-and-over age group, only 4 percent of those in poor health, 11 percent in good health and 17 percent in excellent health were engaged in doing volunteer work. In fact, a larger proportion of people over 80 who defined themselves as in excellent health were volunteers than people between 65 and 79 who were in poor health; close to one in five of the very oldest who were in excellent health were volunteers (not substantially lower than the average in the sample as a whole), compared to only about one in ten of the two middle groups who were in poor health.

Table 4–1
Percentage of Respondents Who Volunteer by Age, Controlling for Perceived Health
(n = 2,069)

	Age				Significance		
Perceived Health	60 to 65[a]	65 to 69[b]	70 to 79[c]	80 and over[d]	x^2	df	p
Poor	21 (47)	10 (123)	12 (203)	4 (85)	10.5	3	.01
Good	32 (77)	22 (226)	17 (304)	11 (111)	15.5	3	.001
Excellent	37 (125)	37 (319)	32 (331)	17 (118)	16.7	3	<.001

Note: Numbers in parentheses indicate number out of total sample who fall in that age and perceived health category.
[a] $x^2 = 3.8$, 2 df, p not significant.
[b] $x^2 = 37.2$, 2 df, p = <.001.
[c] $x^2 = 33.8$, 2 df, p = .001.
[d] $x^2 = 9.0$, 2 df, p = .001.

*Is the Lower Volunteer Participation of Retirees
Due to Poorer Health?*

Perhaps the most unexpected finding reported so far is that total retirement does not lead to a greater level of involvement in doing volunteer work. One reason for this might be that retirees are in poorer health than people who are still working. In fact, people often retire because of poor health. For this reason, the association between volunteering and employment status was reexamined in view of the fact that the lower level of participation of retirees might mainly be due to the fact that they are in poorer health than older people who continue to work.

The lower tendency to volunteer when people are fully retired is, to some extent, due to the fact that they tend to be in poorer health than those in other groups. When people defining their health in similar terms are compared, the fully retired do volunteer about as often as people who are still working. For example, among people who were in excellent health, 31 percent of the fully retired and 33 percent of those still working were volunteers. However, a far higher proportion of semiretired people in excellent health, 44 percent were volunteers. Again, it is important to consider these findings in another way; one would expect that the fully retired in excellent health would have more time to volunteer than people who are still working. The data continue to confirm the fact that, regardless of age or health status, total retirement does not result in higher levels of volunteer participation among older people.

Summary

Volunteer participation among older people is affected by increasing age as well as by declining health. These findings are consistent with earlier studies of the social participation and activity levels of older people. The strong impact of increasing age does not begin, however, until after the age of 77. After that, people are far less likely to volunteer and the definition of their health status no longer appears to influence whether or not they engage in volunteering.

The decline in social activity after the age of 77, irrespective of health, suggests that people may, in effect, "retire" from some social activities. Social policies and programs designed to increase older people's involvement in various sorts of social, recreational, and volunteer activities should especially target their efforts toward this older age group insofar as their decreased involvement is not due to less favorable health.

Declining health and increasing age also do not explain why total retirement does not lead to a significantly higher level of participation in volunteering. Subsequent chapters will continue to unravel this perplexing finding, that an objective increase in having more free time, which should occur during retirement, does not lead to an increase in the tendency to be involved in doing volunteer work.

Notes

1. L.K. George and L.B. Bearon, *Role Transitions in Later Life* (Monterey, Calif.: Brooks/Cole, 1980), p. 10.

2. ACTION, op. cit., p. 4. A.P. Karelitz, *Voluntarism and Some Major Life Changes* (University of Pittsburgh Center for Urban Research, 1976). P. Taietz and O.F. Larson, "Social Participation and Old Age," *Rural Sociology,* 1956, Vol. 21, p. 233.

3. For a review of these studies, see Palmore, op. cit., pp. 47–49.

4. Ibid., p. 47.

5. G. Maddox, "Activity and Morale: A Longitudinal Study of Selected Elderly Subjects," *Social Forces,* 1963, Vol. 42, No. 2, pp. 195–204.

6. Palmore, op. cit., p. 43.

7. Taietz and Larson, op. cit., p. 232.

8. F.C. Jeffers and C.R. Nichols, "The Relationship of Activities and Attitudes to Physical Well-Being in Older People," in E. Palmore, ed., *Normal Aging* (Durham, N.C.: Duke University Press, 1970), pp. 304–9.

9. P.M. Keith, "Life Changes, Leisure Activities, and Well-Being among Very Old Men and Women," *Activities, Adaptation, and Aging,* 1982, Vol. 1, No. 1, pp. 67–75.

10. McGuire, op. cit., pp. 19–22.

11. R.M. Coe and E. Barnhill, "Social Participation and Health of the Aged," in A. Rose and W. Peterson, eds., op. cit., p. 216.

12. Hunter and Linn, op. cit., p. 209.

13. C.N. Bull and B. Payne, "The Use of the Older Volunteer: Policy Implications," paper presented at the International Sociological Association Meeting, 1978.

14. S.F. Kornblum, "Impact of a Volunteer Service Role upon Aged People," *Dissertation Abstracts International*, Vol. 43, No. 1, DA-8207595.

15. G. Maddox and E. Douglass, "Self-Assessment of Health: A Longitudinal Study of Elderly Subjects," *Journal of Health and Social Behavior,* 1973, Vol. 14, pp. 87–93.

5

Socioeconomic Status and the Costs and Rewards of Volunteering

A person's income, education, and savings have an important impact on the experience of growing older because they substantially alter the links between role loss, increasing age, declining health, and participation in social life. This is evident in two very different research studies done about twenty years apart which reached similar conclusions. The first one was conducted in 1947–48; 1,300 people living in four rural communities in upstate New York were interviewed. About one-third of them were over 65. This study found that a person's level of participation in formal organizations was mainly due to socioeconomic status and whether or not people were retired. These two factors had a greater influence on declining participation than age.[1] The second study, based on interviews with approximately six thousand men in 1969 and 1971 for the Social Security Administration's Retirement History Survey, also found that socioeconomic status had an important impact on the experience of growing older since it was a stronger predictor of formal and informal social participation than either retirement or widowhood.[2]

What appears to be an effect of age might, instead, be a reflection of differences between generations. Social participation might therefore seem to decline with age but instead actually be a reflection of the fact that older people are less educated and have lower incomes than younger people. Cutler observed that "if older people had the same socioeconomic characteristics as younger or middle age persons, we would expect to see membership levels as high or higher than those of middle age persons."[3]

The decline in volunteering that appears to be due to increasing age and declining health merits another look since, like social participation in general, levels of volunteering might look as if they are affected by aging and by declining health but might instead be due to generational differences. Older people might have lower social participation than younger people because the occupations open to them when they entered the labor force were the kinds now held by people who are less often involved in volunteering and in voluntary associations— service or blue collar jobs. Since there has been an expansion of employment in white collar jobs, especially professional jobs, during this century, changes in the structure of the labor force could also account for generational differences in levels of volunteering. This chapter looks at the importance of education, income, and occupation for volunteering within the older population. It also considers whether the high level of participation by people who are semiretired is due to the fact that they are better educated and in more prestigious occupations than people who are fully retired. Several possible reasons for social class differences in volunteering are also considered.

Review of the Literature

Social Class in Research on Older People

A considerable amount of research has focused on social class differences in all age groups. Far less has been done on the importance of social class in the older population, but the existing research on this topic has some important insights. Social gerontologists have looked at the importance of social class in the older population in three different ways. A number of studies have focused on economic well-being in the older population in order to estimate the size and the proportion of older people who are either living in poverty or who are economically independent.[4] Of particular concern is the impact of retirement on the incomes of people in different social strata. A second focus is whether or not there are social class differences in the ways people adjust to widowhood and to retirement. Finally, there has been some attention to the connection between social status and the ways older people allocate their leisure time, especially the effect of class on membership in voluntary associations.

Effects of Socioeconomic Status on Widowhood and Retirement

Women in different social classes respond differently to widowhood. Better-educated women with higher incomes fare relatively better when they become widowed: they have higher levels of well-being and are also more socially active.[5] Lopata reaches the conclusion that women with more education are better at analyzing situations objectively and modifying their own behavior if it is directed toward unrealistic and unattainable goals. These abilities enable them to more successfully adapt to the changes that accompany widowhood.[6]

There is a great deal of research on the retirement experiences of people at different social class levels. Much of this research is pertinent for understanding correlates of volunteering. It focuses on two major consequences of retirement: first, the fact that it results in a reduction in income; and, second, the impact of no longer having the frustrations, the gratification, or the daily social contacts that work provides.

The typical retiree's income is about one-half of what it was before retirement.[7] There are some substantial class variations in the actual financial impact of retirement and on people's perception of whether or not their after-retirement income is adequate. A recent study based on two large samples (those of the Retirement History Survey and National Longitudinal Survey) looked at these issues and found that retirement had virtually no effect on actual or perceived incomes of those who had been in the lowest income group. For those whose incomes had been in the highest third before retirement, there was a reduction in income, but relatively few of them defined their postretirement income as inadequate. Retirement had the most significant impact on the middle group whose incomes declined more than the two other groups' after retirement and who more often felt their retirement incomes were inadequate.[8] The effect of retirement on income is not a uniform one across social strata; it has a greater impact on retirees who had been in the middle income group.

There are also some significant differences in people's attitudes toward retirement. A 1982 survey sponsored by the American Association of Retired Persons (AARP) included several questions designed to tap people's feelings about being retired. There are striking differences in responses between income groups. About one in three retirees with incomes of less than $4,000 per year were glad they had retired. This is much lower than for the most affluent group, with incomes of $18,000 or more. Four-fifths of affluent retirees were glad to be retired.[9]

Retirement is more usually described as the loss of a social role rather than a transition from one social status to another. The implication is that this loss is a negative experience. For many people, this may not at all be the case—in fact, the reverse could be true. Retirement may be a more positive experience than working. Work may not have provided gratification. Thus, retirement could be a welcomed event not because it allows a person to engage in leisure but because it frees them from work. Indeed, people with more education and higher-status occupations prefer to continue to work for a longer time.[10] The control over retirement also appears greater for higher-status workers. They tend to plan more and prepare more[11] and also tend to be more able to retire at the age that they select.[12] Compared to others, workers in higher-status jobs are probably pulled into retirement rather than pushed out of the labor force.

It is commonly assumed that people in more prestigious occupations continue to work for a longer portion of their lives because they are more satisfied with their jobs. There is, however, no empirical support for these assumptions. Three studies concerned with the relationship between occupation and when people retire[13] and an extensive review of studies of adjustment to retirement[14] have all found that occupation does not have a great impact on when people retire. The review concluded that "the relationship between occupational level, orientations to work and attitudes toward retirement is relatively cloudy and requires further research."[15]

Social Participation and Social Class

At all age levels, there is a close correspondence between people's levels of social involvement and their social class. People with higher social status tend to belong to a larger number of voluntary associations,[16] and they are more involved in political activities[17] as well as in volunteer work.[18]

These associations also occur in the older population. Two detailed reviews of studies of older people's social participation reach the conclusion that social class does affect participation in a variety of formal activities for members of this age group.[19] In contrast, it is not clear whether or not class influences two sorts of informal social relationships (contact with friends and contact with relatives). Some of the research shows either no class differences or more family contact in the lower social strata.[20]

It is important to consider why social class affects social and leisure activities for people at all age levels, and if the impact of socioeconomic status is different for older people since their social interaction often occurs within the context of retirement and widowhood. This subject is one facet of a larger issue: that social standing is related to the ways people allocate their time throughout the life cycle and also during the time when they face the changes that are part of the aging process.

The connection between class and leisure reflects both differences in taste and in economic resources. For older people on relatively fixed incomes, it especially reflects differences in the amount of money people can spend.[21] It costs far more money to travel than to watch television. Even a trip to a public library or a senior center is more accessible to people who can afford to pay for them without appreciably affecting how they could spend money for other things.

Social Class Differences in Volunteering

Social class position strongly influences whether or not people do some type of volunteer work and also the kinds of jobs they do when they volunteer. These associations exist also for older people,[22] although the relationship between social class and the types of volunteer jobs done by older people has not been looked at very closely. Recent large-scale surveys of patterns of volunteering by older people show that people who are better educated, who are more affluent, and who are (or who were) in more prestigious jobs have a greater tendency to do volunteer work. These relationships exist regardless of how volunteering is defined in the research, whether people are asked about interest in volunteering, and whether "formal volunteering" or a broader definition is used (as in studies conducted by Gallup which were sponsored by Independent Sector).[23] Social class was not a factor that distinguished between older people who are engaged in doing volunteer work and their contemporaries who spend time in other forms of leisure.[24]

Implications of Previous Research

Older people's lives are shaped by their social class in several very important ways. First is the experience of retiring and the process of adjusting to retirement. Second, people choose different sorts of activities when they retire and, therefore, social class influences whether people spend time doing volunteer work. This chapter explores the connection between volunteering and social standing. It also reexamines whether some of the associations already discussed—the effects of age and health on volunteering—are greatly altered by social class differences within the older population.

Measuring Social Class in the Older Population

Most studies of social stratification use a composite index of social position which combines income, education, and occupation. This is done in order to take into account that these three dimensions of social standing are highly correlated with each other but should be measured separately in order to provide more sensitive measurements of socioeconomic status. In contrast to this procedure, each one of the indicators of social position is used individually in this book; there are several reasons why this procedure was adopted. First, the connection between income and the two other measures of socioeconomic status becomes weaker over the life cycle. This change is especially apparent after the age of seventy. Spearman correlation coefficients were computed for the entire study population, including people who were under the age of 60. The over-60 group was divided into three groups (60 to 69, 70 to 79, and 80 and over). For the under-60 group, the correlation between income and education was strong ($r = .42$) and highly significant ($p < .001$). Although still significant, it declined for respondents in each subsequent decade of life. For those who were 80 and over, the correlation was far smaller ($r = .06$) but nonetheless still significant. A similar pattern occurred for income and occupation. The associations remained significant for all the age groups but were far higher for the under-60 group ($r = .35$) than for those in their sixties ($r = .28$) or seventies ($r = .22$) or who were over 80 ($r = .10$).

The links between income, education, and occupation become weaker in the older population for several reasons. When some older people remain in the labor force, they might work in occupations different from those that they held during most of their worklives. This might be a by-product of discrimination in employment and a reflection of the fact that some older workers have to accept jobs with lower status and lower pay than the jobs they held during most of their worklives in order to continue to work. Some older people may, for these reasons, experience downward occupational mobility. A major study of men's employment patterns concluded that older displaced workers did, in fact, "slide down the occupational ladder" when they found new jobs.[25]

The data in this study population do not confirm the existence of downward occupational mobility since the link between education and current or former occupation remains about the same for all four age groups. However, the declining link between occupation and income suggests that other factors influence retirement income. Older people's incomes are related to their occupations (since the correlations are significant), but are also affected by other factors such as union membership, type of industry, and whether or not a person worked for a small business or a large corporation. Income differences clearly narrow during old age. A retired automobile worker might have a higher income than a former college professor.

Since the connections between the three indicators of social position—income, education, and occupation—become weaker during old age, the analysis departs from a standard procedure in sociological research. Rather than using one index that combines all three, each one is considered separately. Another reason for this procedure is that about one in eight respondents had been homemakers and, therefore, had no occupational status.

Findings

The three indicators of social position—educational achievement, income, and occupation—are clearly associated with involvement in doing volunteer work. (See table 5–1.) This finding is consistent with other studies that show that there is a positive relationship between social status and various types of formal social participation.

There are striking differences in the proportion of people with different levels of schooling who are volunteers. Less than one in ten with fewer than nine years of education did volunteer work compared to about one in four high school graduates and close to half of college graduates. A similar progression occurs for people in various occupations. About one in ten farmers, one in eight unskilled blue collar and service workers, one-quarter of clerical workers, one-third of sales workers, proprietors, and managers, and four in ten professionals were engaged in volunteering.

Differences between income categories are also substantial, although not as striking as for educational and occupational groups. All respondents with incomes of $15,000 or more were combined into one category since there were no differences in the levels of participation for people with higher incomes. The findings are quite similar to a study conducted in 1981 by NRTA-AARP (the National Retired Teacher's Association and the American Association of Retired Persons) in which 1,001 people over the age of 55 were asked about their involvement as volunteers. About one-fifth of respondents with incomes of $8,000 or less were volunteers compared to one-third with moderate incomes ($8,000 to $18,000) and 38 percent with high incomes of $18,000 or more.

Table 5–1
Associations between Volunteer Participation and Indicators of Socioeconomic Status

Indicator of Socioeconomic Status	Did Volunteer Work				Significance		
	Yes		No				
	%	n	%	n	x^2	df	p
Educational achievement (n = 2,069)					170.6	4	<.001
1 to 8 years	9	45	91	428			
9 to 11 years	17	116	83	570			
High school graduate	26	106	74	307			
Some college	38	104	62	172			
College graduate or more	47	104	53	117			
Current or former occupation (n = 1,729)					93.2	8	<.001
Professional	41	99	59	140			
Manager	33	47	67	94			
Small business proprietor	35	18	65	33			
Sales	33	35	67	71			
Clerical	26	56	74	159			
Skilled blue collar	20	32	80	128			
Operative/unskilled	16	59	84	314			
Service	16	53	84	284			
Farm owner/worker	11	12	89	95			
Annual household income (n = 1,755)					77.1	3	<.001
Less than $6,999	14	106	86	639			
$7,000 to $9,999	23	70	77	233			
$10,000 to $14,999	30	87	70	208			
$15,000 or more	36	148	64	246			

There are, then, substantial differences within the older population based on education, occupation, and, to a lesser extent, income. These patterns are probably continued from earlier periods in life since they greatly affect levels of participation at all age levels.

Why Is Social Status Associated with Volunteering?

One important difference between older and younger volunteers is that older people are probably less often motivated by family- and job-related reasons for volunteering, issues explored in some depth in the next chapter. The meaning of doing volunteer work therefore probably changes a great deal as a person ages. No longer is a person involved because it affects one's children (as occurs when volunteering for a child's school or for a scouting group) or because it is expected in one's job. Instead, the nature of the volunteer job itself and the gratification derived from it probably become more important during old age.

A great number of studies document a strong connection between various forms of social participation and socioeconomic status. This occurs at all age levels. People with higher occupations, more education, and higher incomes are more involved in volunteering and in voluntary associations. Very few studies attempt to explain why this relationship occurs. Several reasons are presented here and in the last chapter.

The most compelling reason for the connection between volunteering and higher social status is economic: people with higher social status have greater financial resources. Participation in volunteering and in voluntary associations costs time as well as money. Time spent in volunteering could otherwise be used for other leisure pursuits. A person could also use this time to work and thereby acquire additional income.[26] There are tangible costs that may reduce the chances that some low-income people spend time as volunteers throughout their lives but especially during old age: the costs of transportation and meals away from home. In addition to the direct costs of volunteering, or the income that might have been earned during that time, there are indirect costs as well. For example, the cost of having clothing appropriate for a work setting may be a significant consideration for retirees and for homemakers.

In addition to the costs of volunteering, the rewards may also differ according to a person's socioeconomic status. Higher-status volunteers may be more attractive to organizations because of the job skills and personal contacts they have, the latter being of special importance in fundraising. People with higher social status are more concentrated in the kinds of volunteer jobs that offer significant rewards and prestige—as officers and as board members. In contrast, volunteers with less status are more often assigned to clerical tasks or provide direct services to individuals.[27] These are the kinds of jobs in which people are more prone to burnout when they are paid; there is no reason to think that burnout is less likely when a person is a part-time volunteer rather than a full-time worker. Future researchers might explore whether the assignment of volunteers to particular jobs mirrors people's position in the class structure. The association between socioeconomic status and social participation probably has a great deal to do with the ways volunteers and members of organizations are assigned to jobs on the basis of who they are. Class differences in volunteering has a great deal to do with the kinds of skills and abilities the volunteer can offer as well as the types of jobs to which the volunteer might be assigned.

Occupational Differences in Access to Semiretirement

Perhaps the most striking finding of this book has been that semiretired people have a significantly higher tendency to be involved in doing volunteer work than people who continue to be working or who are completely retired. This finding might be due to occupational differences since people who are more likely to volunteer at any age—those who are better educated and in higher-status occupations—are also more able to be semiretired. Older professionals in the sample were far more likely to be working (27 percent) than those who had been managers (21 percent), clerical or blue collar workers. Older professionals apparently have more access to part-time work, presumably using their job skills, than people from other types of jobs.

Since the higher participation of people who were semiretired might be a spurious one, due instead to the fact that the semiretired are a group that tends to be concentrated in high-status occupations, the original association between volunteering and employment status was reconsidered in light of occupational differences. Four broad occupational categories were created combining jobs with fairly similar levels of prestige and participation in volunteering.

The higher participation of the semiretired is not due to their concentration in higher-status occupations. For two of the four groups considered, semiretired people volunteer far more often than either people who are employed or those who are fully retired. Among professionals, 34 percent of the employed and 40 percent of the fully retired were involved in doing some type of volunteer work. In contrast, 67 percent of professionals who were semiretired were volunteers. These differences are statistically significant ($x^2 = 7.4$, $df = 2$, $p = .01$). For clerical and skilled blue collar workers, total retirement has little effect since an equal proportion of workers and retirees are volunteers (23 percent). Participation by the semiretired is much greater (38 percent). Different patterns occur for the two other groups. Among managers, proprietors, and sales workers, employment status is unrelated to participation. For operative, service, and farm workers, the employed and semiretired volunteer equally often (20 percent and 19 percent, respectively), which is somewhat more than the fully retired (14 percent).

People who work during retirement are far more likely to be doing volunteer work than people who are completely retired. This finding is not due to the fact that the semiretired might be younger, view themselves as being in better health, or be in occupations more amenable to semiretirement. Subsequent chapters will continue to reexamine this relationship and will consider some other explanations.

Age, Health, and Socioeconomic Status

One reason offered for the lower level of social participation by older people is that they are less educated than younger people. What appears, then, to be a decline in participation because of either age or poorer health may, instead, be due to the fact that older people are less involved in a variety of social and leisure pursuits not because they are old, but because they are less educated. Another reason, closely related but nonetheless distinct, is that older people tend to be in occupations where lower participation is more common. They tend to be in different sorts of occupations than younger people not only because they are less educated but because of the types of job opportunities available to them when they first began to work.

To consider whether increasing age and declining health are real reasons for declining participation or are merely due to occupational and educational differences between age groups, the associations between volunteering, age, and perceived health were reexamined in light of socioeconomic differences.

The correlations between volunteering and age or perceived health are reduced when socioeconomic factors are controlled. However, the associations continue to exist. The original correlation between age and volunteering was $r = -.14$. When the three indicators of socioeconomic status (education, occupation, and income) are introduced, the correlation between volunteering and age is reduced. However, the association between volunteering and age continues to be a significant one ($r = .10$). The same occurs in the relationship between volunteering and perceived health. The zero-order correlation is .20 and the partial correlation is .10 when the three measures of socioeconomic status are controlled.

Socioeconomic differences within the older population do play a role in declining participation. However, at the same time, increasing age and declining health greatly affect participation.

Summary

Older people vary greatly in their tendency to be involved in volunteer work because of their education, their occupations, and their incomes. These differences occur at all age levels and continue into old age. Several reasons for this association are offered. First, volunteering costs time and money. Second, the actual experiences of volunteers and the rewards they receive probably vary according to class. Higher-status volunteers are assigned more prestigious jobs offering them the ability to set policy whereas volunteers with lower social status are more concentrated in less prestigious and perhaps less interesting jobs, the kinds of jobs in which people are more likely to burn out even when they are paid workers.

A major finding described thus far—that retirement is not associated with an increased tendency to be involved in volunteer work—was reexamined for various occupational groups. Once again, there was no evidence that total retirement was associated with a higher level of involvement in doing volunteer work for any occupational group. Indeed, being semiretired was associated with a greater tendency to be a volunteer for professionals and clerical workers as well as for skilled blue collar workers.

A third area of concern was whether or not declining participation within the older population could be a result of socioeconomic differences rather than due to the effects of increasing age or of declining health. This has been suggested as a reason why older people might appear to be less active when they are compared to younger people. However, the data show that increasing age and declining health account for decreasing participation in old age. Socioeconomic variables reduce, but do not eliminate these relationships.

Notes

1. P. Taietz and O. Larson, op. cit., pp. 229–38.
2. T. Wan and B. Odell, "Major Role Losses and Social Participation of Older Males," *Research on Aging,* 1983, Vol. 5, No. 2, pp. 173–96.
3. S.J. Cutler, "Age Differences in Voluntary Association Membership," *Social Forces,* 1976, Vol. 55, No. 1, p. 55.
4. Upp, op. cit. See also M. Moon, "The Incidence of Poverty among the Aged," *Journal of Human Resources,* 1979, Vol. 14, No. 2, pp. 211–21; and H.L. Sheppard and R.E. Mantovani, *Aging in the Eighties: Hard-Strapped and Well-Off Retirees: A Study in Perceived Income Adequacy* (Washington, D.C.: National Council on the Aging, 1982).
5. L.K. George, *Role Transitions in Later Life* (Monterey, Calif.: Brooks/Cole, 1980), p. 92.
6. Lopata, op. cit., pp. 268–69.
7. Streib and Schneider, op. cit., p. 92.
8. G.G. Fillenbaum, L.K. George, and E.B. Palmore, "Determinants and Consequences of Retirement among Men of Different Races and Economic Levels," *Journal of Gerontology,* 1985, Vol. 40, No. 1, p. 92.
9. American Association of Retired Persons, Research and Data Resources Unit, "Employment and Retirement among Older Americans," *Data Gram* (Washington, D.C.: AARP, 1983).
10. B. McPherson and N. Guppy, "Pre-retirement Life-Style and the Degree of Planning for Retirement," *Journal of Gerontology,* 1979, Vol. 34, No. 2, p. 258. See also C.L. Rose and J.M. Mogey, "Aging and Preference for Later Retirement," *Aging and Human Development,* 1972, Vol. 3, p. 54; I.H. Simpson, K.W. Back, and J.C. McKinney, "Exposure to Information on, Preparation for, and Self-Evaluation in Retirement," in I.H. Simpson and J.C. McKinney, eds., *Social Aspects of Aging* (Durham, N.C.: Duke University Press, 1966), pp. 90–105.
11. McPherson and Guppy, op. cit. Simpson et al., op. cit.
12. S.H. Beck, "Position in the Economic Structure and Unexpected Retirement," *Research on Aging,* Vol. 5, No. 2, p. 211.
13. E.A. Friedman and R.J. Havighurst, "Retirement from Work to Play," in E. Friedman and R.J. Havighurst, eds., *The Meaning of Work and Retirement* (Chicago: University of Chicago Press, 1954). See also Rose and Mogey, op. cit.
14. J. Howard, J. Marshall, P. Rechnitzer, D. Cunningham, and A. Donner, "Adapting to Retirement," *Journal of the American Geriatrics Society,* 1982, Vol. 30, No. 8, pp. 488–500.
15. Ibid., p. 493.
16. R.W. Hodge and D.J. Treiman, "Social Participation and Social Status," *American Sociological Review,* 1968, Vol. 33, pp. 722–39. See also J. Houghland,

K. Kyong-Dong, and J. Christenson, "The Effects of Ecological and Socioeconomic Status Variables on Membership and Participation in Voluntary Organizations," *Rural Sociology,* 1979, Vol. 44, No. 3, pp. 602–12.

17. See Cutler, "Aging and Voluntary Association Participation," op. cit., p. 470.

18. ACTION, op. cit., p. 6. Gallup, op. cit., p. 13.

19. Palmore, op. cit., p. 55. Riley and Foner, op. cit., p. 505.

20. Palmore, op. cit., p. 55. See also R.W. Kernodle and R.L. Kernodle, "The Differential Use of Social Life Space of the Retired Elderly by Social Class," paper presented at the Annual Meeting of the Southern Sociological Society, 1978.

21. S. Parker, "Leisure and the Elderly," *Society and Leisure,* 1973, Vol. 5, No. 4, p. 53.

22. American Association of Retired Persons, "Older Americans and . . . Volunteerism" (Washington, D.C.: AARP, n.d.). See also S.M. Chambré, "The Influences of Class and Gender on Volunteer Participation of the Elderly," paper presented at the Conference on Nonprofit Leadership and Management, 1984, Boston, Mass.; and Ventura and Worthy, op. cit., p. 12.

23. Lambert, op. cit. Monk and Cryns, op. cit.

24. Dye et al., op. cit., p. 217. Hunter and Linn, op. cit., p. 207. Mellinger and Holt, op. cit., p. 451.

25. H.S. Parnes, ed., *Work and Retirement: A Longitudinal Study* (Cambridge, Mass.: MIT Press, 1981), p. 75.

26. P. Menchik and B. Weisbrod, "Government Crowding Out and Contributions of Time—Or, Why Do People Work for Free?" (unpublished paper, n.d.). See also V. Schram and M. Dunsing, "Influences on Married Women's Volunteer Work Participation," *Journal of Consumer Research,* 1980, Vol. 7, pp. 372–79.

27. Chambré, 1984, op. cit.

6
Volunteering and the Diminishing Importance of Gender: Patterns of Participation among Older Men and Women

An understanding of the meaning of volunteering for older men and women requires some attention to the historical context in which they grew up and spent their lives. People who were over the age of 60 in 1981 were all born before 1921. This age group actually consists of people who belong to several different generations; the very oldest were born in the final decades of the past century.

Despite generational differences, all of them grew up and spent most of their adult lives in a society that defined men's and women's places in the family, in the labor force, and in society in general to be very different from each other. Men mainly derived their identity from being breadwinners. Women were primarily expected to be homemakers; if they did work, it was for economic reasons.[1]

The proper roles for men and women, while still distinct, have become redefined in the past several decades, which has begun to have an impact on the composition of the older population. Men are generally more involved in performing household tasks, and more and more women are spending significant portions if not virtually all of their lives in the paid labor force. Changes in the sex roles for men and for women occurred at different stages in the life cycles of today's older population. The emergence of different work patterns for women and changes in some men's family responsibilities did accelerate when the very youngest in the sample were in their forties and when the oldest were already in their midsixties.

The clearest evidence of these changes is the increasing number of older women who are retirees rather than homemakers. Only one-quarter of the women in this sample were homemakers and most of the women, well over two-thirds, described themselves as being either fully retired (64 percent) or semiretired (5 percent). The percentage of women who were homemakers was even smaller in a survey that included a wider age range, people over the age of 55: only one in five women were homemakers.[2]

Volunteering has been especially viewed as the province of women, particularly women who are homemakers. Changes in work patterns have two very significant implications. First, they may reduce women's involvement in volunteering and, as a byproduct, decrease the supply of volunteers. Surprising as it may seem, very little research has been done on the general subject of women as volunteers and the more specific issue of the effect of changes in women's work patterns on their involvement in volunteering. What does exist is suggestive that when women work, they decrease their involvement in voluntary associations[3] and are less often involved in volunteering because women who earn salaries are not willing to work without any pay.[4]

The Harris survey, because of its size, permits a detailed investigation of volunteering among older men and women. It is possible to look at some similarities within and between the two gender categories with regard to their current employment situation, occupations, income levels, and family involvement. Some findings on gender differences in old age are presented in order to frame the analysis.

Gender Differences in Retirement

The separate definitions of men's and women's roles—that men are breadwinners and women are homemakers—is reflected in most research on the aging experience of older men and women. Researchers have looked at the effects of retirement on men and the impact of widowhood on women. Studies of retirement have been based on samples of men; research on widowhood has focused on women.[5] Since women were considered to be family-centered and to lack a significant commitment to work, it was generally thought that the major change for women as they aged was becoming widowed. For men, the major change in their lives was thought to be retirement, an event described as a "crisis." Retirement was not seen as a crisis for women as it was for men. Widowhood was said to mark the major change for women in old age but was termed a problematic event for men.

Another theme in the gerontological literature has been that sex role differences become blurred during old age and that men and women become androgynous.[6] This view is consistent with traditional sex roles because men and women were both losing the major roles that distinguished them. This may have been accurate at earlier points in history since retirement from the paid labor force was not a common experience for older women and widowhood is still less common for men than for women since women tend to outlive men. When men lose a spouse, they have a better chance of remarrying since there are many more older women than older men.

Changes in gender roles have led to a greater amount of interest in differences between older men and older women. There is a substantial amount of recent research on this topic, but it is difficult to draw valid conclusions because many of the studies are based on small, cross-sectional samples. However, their conclusions do contradict some previous ideas about the impacts of retirement on women and of widowhood on men, while, in general, they provide little support for the view that old age is a time of androgyny.

Men and women have different experiences during old age. They vary in their attitudes toward retirement,[7] in the ways they plan, prepare and adjust to retirement,[8] and also in the sorts of activities they pursue while they are retired.[9] Several studies have indeed found that women's ties to work are far stronger than was assumed and that women are more negative about retirement than men are.[10] Indeed, retirement is as much, if not more, of a crisis for women as it is for men. Finally, research on men's experiences as widowers also casts some light on the fact that for those men who do become widowed, it marks some important changes in their lives as well.

Friendship, Social Participation, and Leisure Activities of Older Men and Women

Older men and women tend to have dissimilar sorts of social relationships with their friends and their families. They also differ in the number of voluntary associations they join and how much time they spend with them. Women join voluntary associations that are mainly composed of other women.[11] Another difference is that men and women choose to be involved in different sorts of leisure activities.[12] Many, if not most of these differences represent a continuation of gender differences that have existed throughout their lives.

At all ages, men are more involved in goal-oriented, instrumental roles whereas women spend more energy developing intimate social relationships, roles that can be described as expressive and deal with the social and the emotional aspects of human relationships. Women's involvements in both informal social relationships and voluntary associations have generally been thought to be consistent with and even extensions of family roles.[13]

These differences in style continue into old age and have an appreciable impact on the ways older men and women adapt to old age. One of the earliest books on the aging process, which was published more than twenty years ago, identified two major types of adjustment patterns. Some older people exhibited what was called a "gessellschaft" pattern: they were more involved in secondary social relationships and had more involvement in task-oriented and relatively impersonal social relationships. The other was the "gemeinschaft" style, a form where the dominant social relationships were primary, personal, and not oriented to any specific set of goals. The researchers found that the gesellschaft pattern was mostly composed of men (71 percent); two-thirds of the gemeinschaft group was female.[14]

Men and women also exhibit different patterns of friendships throughout life continuing into old age.[15] Men have a larger number of friends, but women's relationships are more intimate.[16] Men's friendships are often based on common experiences, a kind of relationship that has been described as "mateship."[17]

Men and women probably respond differently to the experience of being widowed. Widowhood affects their social relationships in some very different ways. Men spend less time with other people when they lose a spouse, but for women, widowhood has less of an impact. Married women and widows had similar levels of social interaction.[18] Another study looked at the effects of widowhood on different types of social relationships and found that widowed men actually visited friends more frequently than married men.[19]

To gain some perspective on these findings, it is important to consider the way men and women perceive leisure time during old age and how they allocate their leisure time. Older women believe that they have less free time than older men think they have,[20] and they use their time differently. Men spend more time doing household maintenance whereas women are more involved in doing handwork.[21]

Since volunteering is probably closely linked to participation in voluntary associations, it is important to consider how older men and women differ in the forms and nature of their participation. The evidence is contradictory. Some studies reach the conclusion that the higher level of participation by men continues into old age and that older men are significantly more involved in voluntary associations than older women.[22] Several more recent studies, however, have found that older men and women have quite similar patterns of participation.[23] There is also some evidence that the aging process affects men's and women's affiliations differently and that older women tend to decrease their participation more sharply as they age than do older men.[24]

Volunteering and Gender

Even though men are more involved in voluntary associations, women have usually been more involved in doing volunteer work. A strong image of the typical volunteer is of a woman, particularly a married woman who is a home-maker. This view, while never entirely accurate, was a major conclusion in the first major report on volunteers in the United States, the *Americans Volunteer* survey done by the U.S. Department of Labor.[25] People who were interviewed as part of the April 1965 Current Population Survey were asked if they did any type of volunteer work. A major limitation of the method used was that volunteering did not include work for religious organizations. The typical volunteer was a married homemaker whose involvement was often an extension of her maternal role—she worked as a teacher's aide or with a scouting group.

Several more recent studies have shown that even though women's involvement in volunteering is closely linked to their role as mothers, other important interests and motivations do come into play. When younger women volunteer, it is in the interests of their children but also in their own interests. Even in fairly traditional volunteer roles, such as Girl Scout leader, women volunteer so that they can take a leadership role.[26] Homemakers also volunteer in order to improve their future position in the labor market since unpaid work provides an opportunity to acquire new job skills and to practice old skills.[27] For many, volunteering is a way to be assured of having social interaction with other adults and to acquire an identity other than being "just a housewife."[28]

Women's participation in volunteering has been commonly assumed to be an extension of their maternal role. The patterns and meaning of volunteering for other groups is relatively less understood. One purpose here is to explore some of these issues further and to compare the findings in this sample with other studies.

Findings

Levels of Participation of Older Men and Women

A common view in our society, and in some of the writing on the subject as well, is that volunteering is the province of women, especially women who are homemakers. The patterns of participation by the men and women in this sample do not confirm that this is still true, since an almost identical proportion of men and women were volunteers. In fact, the proportion was slightly higher for men than for women: 24 percent of the men and 22 percent of the women in the sample were volunteers.

This finding might at first seem surprising since most older volunteers appear to be women. There is a difference, however, between looking at the *likelihood* of volunteering and the *composition* of the older population involved in volunteering. Older men and older women have about an equal tendency to be involved in volunteering. However, most older volunteers are women: 55 percent of them are women and 45 percent are men. This occurs, of course, because the bulk of the older population (57 percent of this sample) are women.

At first, the finding that men and women are equally likely to be involved in volunteering might seem to be due to the fact that men and women become more similar in old age. When compared to other recent studies, however, these findings suggest something else. Gender differences in volunteering appear to be diminishing for people at all ages if, in fact, they ever really existed. The results of six studies conducted between 1974 and 1983 illustrate this. In the 1965 survey (the very earliest study to tabulate the proportion of men and women who were volunteers), the difference between the proportion of men and women of all ages who volunteered was much greater than in more recent polls: 22 percent of the women and 16 percent of the men had volunteered some time during the previous year. The 1974 Americans Volunteer survey defined volunteering in broader terms since it included religious volunteering. By then, the male/female difference had narrowed: 19 percent of the men and 21 percent of the women had volunteered over the past year; in the over-60 group, there were much greater differences, as 20 percent of the older men were volunteers as were 26 percent of the older women.[29] Several surveys conducted in the 1980s (including this one) show that the tendency of men and women to participate in volunteering is not as different as it was thought to be and may, in fact, be narrowing. A 1983 survey conducted by Gallup, which defined volunteering more broadly than this one, found that 53 percent of men and 56 percent of women were volunteers.[30] These proportions are much closer than a similar Gallup survey done in 1981, which found that the proportions were 47 percent for men and 56 percent for women.[31]

Effects of Age on Men's and Women's Patterns of Volunteering

Men and women might be equally likely to volunteer because of the effects of age. Since women live longer than men, the sample includes women who tend to be older as a group than the men. The ratio of men to women in the 60-to-65 age group was about equal. In the oldest age category, the 80-and-over group, there were two women for every man.

Even though men and women have similar overall levels of participation in volunteering, there might also be differences within each gender category. Men and women might differ in how their participation changes with age. Some studies have found that men's participation in voluntary associations is more stable than women's.[32] This might also occur for volunteering.

In order to look at possible gender differences, the study population was divided into four age groups in order to look at the proportion of men and women in each group who did some type of volunteer work. The data show that in three of the four age categories, the proportion of men and women doing volunteer work is about equal or is slightly higher for men. For example, in the 65-to-69 group, 29 percent of the men and 25 percent of the women were involved in volunteering. In the 80-and-over group, this changes. Men who are very old are half as likely to be involved in volunteering (7 percent) as women of this age (14 percent). Thus, the similarity in women's and men's participation is not primarily due to age differences.

Another question addressed is whether the declines in participation are similar for men and for women. For people under 80, the pattern is similar for men and for women. After 80, however, the decline is much greater for men. In the 70-to-79 age group, 22 percent of men were volunteers. This declined to 7 percent in the 80-and-over group. For women, 21 percent of the 70-to-79 and 14 percent of the 80-and-over age group were volunteers. These findings contradict several earlier studies of changes in social participation during old age which found greater stability for older men than for older women.

*Effects of Employment Status and Occupation on
Men's and Women's Patterns of Volunteering*

People in various employment categories and in different sorts of occupations do volunteer to a differing extent. When these are combined with gender, the findings are quite interesting. Many studies have found that men are more often members of voluntary groups. Differences in men's and women's employment situations and their occupations may account for this since men and women in jobs with similar levels of prestige have equal levels of voluntary association membership.[33] A study of correlates of volunteering in the over-60 population, based on the 1974 ACTION survey, found that employment status greatly modified gender differences in volunteering and that there was no difference between the proportion of volunteers among men and women who were working. Among retirees, gender differences persisted. Retired women were much more often involved in doing volunteer work (15.5 percent) than retired men (10.7 percent).[34]

With only one exception, men and women in similar employment situations are equally often engaged in volunteer work. That difference is for people who are employed on a full-time basis. For them, 34 percent of the men as compared to 14 percent of the women are also involved in doing volunteer work.

It is also worthwhile to consider the impact of a person's occupation on men's and women's participation since there are major differences between the occupational groups. There is also relatively little known about the retirement experiences of men and women in various occupations. The few studies on this subject focus on men and women in relatively high-status occupations— professionals and people who worked in academic settings.[35]

A four-way cross-tabulation was performed in order to investigate the interrelationships between gender, employment status, occupation, and volunteering. (See table 6–1.) The overall conclusion that can be reached from the table is that men and women are equally involved in volunteering when they are in the same sorts of occupations and in similar employment situations. For example, 33 percent of men and 32 percent of women who were fully retired from sales or management jobs or who had been proprietors were involved in doing volunteer work.

Some notable differences do appear. Working and doing volunteer work appear less compatible for older women in all sorts of jobs. The difference is particularly great among professionals. Professional women who continue to work are far less often involved in doing volunteer work (12 percent) than professional men (50 percent). Among the semiretired, professional women are far less frequently engaged in volunteering (58 percent) than professional men (75 percent). This is not true for women who continue to work in clerical, blue collar, service, and farm jobs who are slightly more likely to be involved as volunteers than men in similar jobs.

Table 6–1
Percentage of Respondents Who Volunteer According to Their Gender, Employment Status, and Current or Former Occupation
(n = 1,729)

Current or Former Occupation	Employed		Semiretired		Fully Retired	
	Men	*Women*	*Men*	*Women*	*Men*	*Women*
Professional	50 (24)	12 (17)	75 (12)	58 (12)	25 (65)	49 (109)
Manager, proprietor, and sales	39 (39)	36 (11)	28 (18)	50 (8)	33 (130)	32 (92)
Clerical and skilled blue collar	20 (20)	25 (24)	42 (12)	33 (12)	21 (145)	24 (162)
Operative, service, unskilled blue collar, and farm	22 (49)	15 (39)	21 (38)	14 (21)	16 (323)	13 (347)

Note: Numbers in parentheses indicate number out of total sample who fall in that occupational, gender, and employment status category.

Retirement seems to have a different impact on the patterns of participation among professional men and women. When professional women retire, their tendency to volunteer increases: 12 percent of professional women who still work are volunteers as compared to 58 percent who are semiretired and 49 percent who retired completely. The pattern is quite different for the professional men. For them, semiretirement is associated with a high level of participation than continuing to work: 50 percent of professional men who never retired at all are volunteers as compared to 75 percent who are semiretired. When professional men retire completely, however, they are far less frequently volunteers; only 25 percent of fully retired men did some type of volunteer work.

Studies of professional men's and women's attitudes toward retirement and their experiences as retirees shed some light on these findings. Professional men view retirement in a negative light and prefer to continue to work as long as possible.[36] When professional men finally retire, it may be at more advanced ages than men in other sorts of occupations. Professional men might wait to retire until neither work nor volunteering are possible because of health reasons. This hypothesis cannot be tested by using the current sample since the question concerning retirement age did not make a distinction between total retirement and semiretirement. One confirmation of this point, however, is that a substantial proportion of male academics were able to continue to work.[37] For professional men, working may, in effect, still be their primary activity when they "retire."

For older women, combining volunteering and work appears far less likely than for older men. A possible explanation for this is that older women in this age group have the major responsibility for household chores. This is only a partial reason, however, since an increase in the potential amount of time women have by retiring does not have much of an impact on the likelihood that most women volunteer. Quite similar proportions of working women and fully retired women in clerical, blue collar, service, and farm jobs are involved in doing volunteer work. It is only for the women in relatively higher status jobs—professionals and managers—that retirement is related to an increased tendency to volunteer. However, once again, we find that total retirement is not related to a substantial increase in volunteering as compared to semiretirement.

These findings again suggest that there are significant status differences in volunteering and that the chances of doing volunteer work are greatly conditioned by the qualities a person brings to a volunteer job. Volunteering is quite uncommon among women who are retired from clerical, blue collar, service, and farm jobs—the kinds of women who are far more numerous than women who have retired from professional and managerial jobs. For such women, and also for men who retire from these sorts of jobs, the small proportion of volunteers represents a continuation of a pattern of a relatively low level of volunteering from the time the person was still working.

If volunteering is a work-substitute, it is mainly for women who are fully retired from jobs as professionals. For older professional men, it appears to complement rather than substitute for work since a sizeable proportion of semiretired professional men are engaged in doing volunteer work. The same occurs for most women since a far greater proportion of women employed part-time (28 percent) or who are semiretired (33 percent) are volunteers than women who are either working full-time (14 percent) or fully retired (23 percent).

Older Homemakers and Volunteering

A common view of volunteers is that many of them are homemakers. This view has two meanings: first, that the bulk of volunteers are homemakers; and, second, that homemakers are more likely to do volunteer work than working women or working men.

The experiences of the people in this sample contradict this stereotype. Homemakers are less likely to volunteer than the women in other employment categories. About one in five homemakers were volunteers compared to 23 percent of fully retired and 33 percent of semiretired women. This finding is a striking one. An extensive review of the literature on this topic revealed that there is relatively little research on patterns of voluntary association membership of older men and women in various employment categories and occupations.

The closest study is an investigation of similarities and differences within and between gender categories for adults of varied ages based on the NORC General Social Survey. When all types of memberships are considered, working and nonworking women had quite similar levels of affiliation after taking into account other factors that influence membership, such as educational achievement. There were significant differences in the types of memberships, however. Working women were more active in instrumental, goal-oriented organizations whereas women who were not employed were more concentrated in organizations having "mixed" goals (that is, they combined social activities with some more specific set of purposes).[38] A second study, one conducted close to forty years ago, compared men and women. However, all of the women included were homemakers. It found that men had higher levels of social participation, but homemakers were more active in religious activities.[39]

Several possible reasons why homemakers were less frequently involved in doing volunteer work were explored. The first explanation considered was whether the previously high participation of homemakers in earlier stages of their lives had led them to become burned out. If this were the case, then homemakers would be overrepresented in the ranks of former volunteers. The survey included a question asking whether nonvolunteers had done volunteer work earlier in their lives. Based on this, the supposition that homemakers had been more active at some earlier time was not supported. About half of the homemakers were former volunteers, which is about the same proportion as among working women and retired women.

A second possibility was that homemakers were less educated than women who had been in the labor force. If this were true, then the lower participation of homemakers might be due to the fact that they were less educated than other women. This is only partly true. Homemakers, working women, and retirees with similar educational levels were compared. The differences did indeed narrow, indicating that a homemakers' lower participation was due to the fact that many of them were less educated than the other women. However, in no category did the homemakers have an appreciably higher level of participation, a finding that might have occurred if homemakers were more active, as they are commonly assumed to be.

Volunteering has especially been viewed as being the province of well-educated and affluent homemakers. Several reasons have been offered for this. First, women in higher social classes are expected to be involved in community service and are given much greater support for such activities than working class women and poor women.[40] Second, more affluent women might be less able to find paid work consistent with their class position. A woman with limited job skills can do an unskilled job as a volunteer and acquire more prestige from doing it than if she performed the same work for pay.[41] For example, working in a hospital gift shop as a volunteer probably confers more prestige than working as a cashier in a store. A third possible reason, which has not been systematically considered elsewhere, is that affluent women can afford to volunteer because they are more able to hire people to perform the routine household tasks that less affluent women would have to do themselves.

Bearing these ideas in mind, we examined whether volunteering is especially the province of higher-status homemakers in the older population. When we consider a characteristic of the woman, her educational level, homemakers who are highly educated do volunteer more than their counterparts with less education: 40 percent of homemakers with some college or more were volunteers compared to 26 percent who were high school graduates, 17 percent with some high school, and 3 percent with eight or fewer years of school. When compared to their counterparts, college-educated homemakers more often volunteered (40 percent) than working women (14 percent), but less often than retired (44 percent) or semiretired (50 percent) women.

The supposition that affluent homemakers have appreciably higher levels of participation is also not confirmed when household incomes of the homemakers are considered. For women with yearly household incomes of less than $15,000, participation is higher for homemakers. About one in ten of the lowest income category ($6,999 or less) were volunteers compared to one in eight with incomes between $7,000 and $9,999. The frequency of participation rises sharply to 41 percent for those in the next category (incomes between $10,000 and $14,999). For homemakers with incomes over $15,000, participation is far lower. One in five of such women were involved in doing volunteer work. This proportion is also low when compared with other affluent women. About one-third of retired women in the highest income group were volunteers, a proportion that is also far higher than the one in five rate for affluent homemakers.

These data indicate that a common view of volunteers is not substantiated in the older population. Affluent women are not overrepresented in the ranks of volunteers. Perhaps the most interesting finding both here and in earlier sections of the chapter when men and women in different occupational categories were examined, is that the retirement of well-educated and affluent women seems to be closely connected to an increase in their participation. When such women are working, they are quite infrequently involved in unpaid work. However, when they retire either partially or totally, they become frequent participants.

Volunteer Participation of Married and Widowed Men and Women

Men and women respond quite differently to the effects of the loss of a spouse. Widows and widowers have very different patterns of social participation. The research on this subject makes quite clear that there are differences between men and women, but many of the results on the nature of these differences are inconsistent. Some researchers have found that women's social participation, was unaffected by the experience of losing a spouse,[42] while another found that widows actually had higher levels of informal social involvement than married women and that married women spent more of their time in passive leisure activities.[43] Widowhood had no influence on men's social interaction in several large-scale surveys,[44] but in another sample, widowers had higher formal and informal social interaction than married men.[45]

In a detailed multivariate analysis of the effects of role loss on older men, Wan and Odell looked at the relative effects of a series of indicators on changes in men's formal and informal social interaction at two points in time. The independent variables included health status, socioeconomic status, prior level of interaction, kin network size, and whether or not the person had become widowed. They found that the loss of the marital role (including both becoming widowed and becoming separated) was less important than other variables. Changes in formal and informal social activity were mainly influenced by two factors: socioeconomic status and previous activity level.[46]

Since men and women adapt differently to old age, I looked at the connection between marriage and volunteering separately for men and for women. A particular interest was whether or not volunteering was a substitute for role loss for women rather than for men. Thus far, this has been the case because women appear to increase their involvement in volunteering when they retire. This does not occur when women become widowed since they are less often (20 percent) volunteers than are currently or formerly married women. Quite similar proportions, about one quarter, of married, never married, and formerly married women are volunteers.

A different pattern emerges for the men. Currently married and formerly married men are significantly more often involved in doing volunteer work (27 percent) than those who became widowed (13 percent) or who had never been married (16 percent).

Since marital status is closely connected to age, it is important to introduce age as a control variable in order to see whether the lower participation of widows was primarily due to the fact that they were older than people who were still married. This is true for most of the women. Widows have similar participation as married women of similar ages. One exception to this was for the very youngest group of women, those between 60 and 64. For them, the participation of married women was far higher (39 percent) than for widows (27 percent). Perhaps many more of these younger widows were working as compared to the married women. Women who become widowed in their fifties are far more likely to reenter the labor force than women who lose a spouse when they are in their sixties or seventies. A recent study based on the 1975 Retirement History survey found that close to one-third of young widows (those between 50 and 60) entered or reentered the labor force after they lost a spouse.

In contrast, only one in ten women began to work if they became widowed between the ages of 61 and 79.[47]

Age has a different effect on the relationship between marital status and volunteering for men. Married men volunteer far more often than widowed men regardless of their ages. For example, one-quarter of married men who were in their seventies did volunteer compared to one-tenth of widowers of a similar age. In the 80-and-over group, however, volunteering is relatively uncommon both for married men (6 percent) as well as for widowers (7 percent). In contrast, about one in eight very old women are involved as volunteers.

Widowhood has a different effect on patterns of volunteering for men and for women. What initially appeared to be a negative effect of widowhood for women was mainly due to age. The loss of a spouse only had a negative impact on the participation of the youngest group of women. For men at all ages, however, widowhood appears to be associated with a reduction in volunteering.

Summary

Gender is a less significant correlate of volunteering than it may have been in the past. Older men and older women show an equal tendency to volunteer. However, there are some very striking gender differences within the older population when other factors are introduced. A man's or woman's employment situation, education, occupation, and marital status greatly affect his or her chances of volunteering. These factors also demonstrate that the experiences of older men and women are nonetheless quite different, but that gender alone does not account for this.

Changes in women's employment patterns over the past twenty years have already begun to influence the composition of the aged population and patterns of volunteering in this age group. The older woman is increasingly a retiree rather than a homemaker. Programs designed for older volunteers should take this very important change into consideration since only about one in ten older volunteers are former homemakers. If volunteering serves as a role substitute for any segment of the older population, then it might perform this function for older women who are retired, especially older women retired from professional and managerial jobs.

Any differences between the volunteer patterns of older men and women seem to have been reduced within the past decade. In 1974, 20 percent of older men and 26 percent of older women were volunteers. Seven years later, in 1981, the proportions were much closer, 24 percent for the men and 22 percent for the women. These patterns mirror a change in the findings of research on voluntary association membership in all age groups and for older men and women since more recent studies show that gender differences are becoming smaller, particularly when men and women in similar employment situations and at similar occupational levels are compared.

There are nonetheless some striking differences between men and women. For men, especially retired professional men, retirement appears to be associated with a significant reduction in the tendency to volunteer whereas for women with similar occupational and educational backgrounds, it appears to serve as a work-substitute.

Notes

1. W. Donahue, H. Orbach, and O. Pollak, "Retirement: The Emerging Social Pattern," in C. Tibbetts, ed., *Handbook of Social Gerontology* (Chicago: University of Chicago Press, 1960), p. 398.

2. American Association of Retired Persons, 1983, op. cit.

3. D.V. Hiller, "Changing Roles for Women: Implications for Community," *American Journal of Community Psychology,* 1981, Vol. 9, No. 4, pp. 387–93.

4. E. Ginzberg, "Life without Work: Does It Make Sense?" in H.S. Parnes, ed., *Policy Issues in Work and Retirement* (Kalamazoo, Mich.: W.E. Upjohn Institute for Employment Research, 1983), p. 30.

5. D. Beeson, "Women in Studies of Aging: A Critique and Suggestion," *Social Problems,* 1975, Vol. 23, pp. 52–55.

6. L.E. Troll and E.M. Parron, "Age Changes in Sex Roles amid Changing Sex Roles: The Double Shift," *Annual Review of Gerontology and Geriatrics,* Vol. 2, pp. 124–28.

7. R.H. Jewson, "After Retirement: An Exploratory Study of the Professional Woman," in M. Szinovacz, ed., *Women's Retirement: Policy Implications of Recent Research* (Beverly Hills, Calif.: Sage, 1982).

8. L.W. Kaye and A. Monk, "Sex Role Traditions and Retirement from Academe," *The Gerontologist,* 1984, Vol. 24, pp. 420–26. N. Kroeger, "Pre-retirement Preparation: Sex Differences in Access, Sources, and Use," in Szinovacz, op. cit. See also E.S. Newman, S.R. Sherman, and C.E. Higgins, "Retirement Expectations and Plans: A Comparison of Professional Men and Women," in Szinovacz, op. cit.

9. Kaye and Monk, op cit.

10. R. Atchley, "Selected Social and Psychological Differences between Men and Women in Later Life," *Journal of Gerontology,* 1976, Vol. 31, No. 2, pp. 204–11. See also D. Jacobson, "Rejection of the Retiree Role: A Study of Female Industrial Workers in their 50's," *Human Relations,* 1974, Vol. 27, No. 5, pp. 477–92.

11. J.M. McPherson and L.S. Lovin, "Sex Segregation in Voluntary Associations," *American Sociological Review,* 1986, Vol. 51, p. 67.

12. F.A. McGuire, "Leisure Time, Activities, and Meanings: A Comparison of Men and Women in Late Life," in N.J. Osgood, ed., *Life After Work,* op. cit.

13. A. Booth, "Sex and Social Participation," *American Sociological Review,* 1972, Vol. 37, pp. 183–92.

14. R.H. Williams and C.G. Wirths, *Lives through the Years* (New York: Atherton, 1965), p. 203.

15. E. Powers and G.L. Bultena, "Sex Differences in Intimate Friendships of Old Age," *Journal of Marriage and the Family,* 1976, Vol. 38, pp. 739–74. See also B.B. Hess, "Sex Roles, Friendship, and the Life Course," *Research on Aging,* Vol. 1, No. 4, pp. 495–515.

16. Booth, op cit. Hess, op cit.
17. L. Rubin, *Just Friends* (New York: Harper & Row, 1985), p. 69.
18. M. Petrowsky, "Marital Status, Sex, and the Social Networks of the Elderly," *Journal of Marriage and the Family,* 1976, Vol. 38, pp. 749–56.
19. P.M. Keith, "Life Changes, Leisure Activities, and Well-Being among Very Old Men and Women," *Activities, Adaptation and Aging,* 1980, Vol. 1, No. 1, p. 71.
20. J. Hoar, "A Study of Free-Time Activities of 200 Aged Persons," *Sociology and Social Research,* 1961, Vol. 45, No. 2, pp. 157–63.
21. Keith, 1980, op. cit., p. 70.
22. Booth, op cit.
23. N. Babchuck, G.R. Peters, D.R. Hoyt, and M.A. Kaiser, "The Voluntary Associations of the Aged," *Journal of Gerontology,* 1979, Vol. 34, No. 4, p. 581. See also S.J. Cutler, "Aging and Voluntary Association Participation," *Journal of Gerontology,* 1977, Vol. 32, No. 4, pp. 470–79.
24. Cutler, "Aging and Voluntary Association Participation," loc. cit.
25. U.S. Department of Labor, *Americans Volunteer,* Manpower/Automation Research Monograph No. 10 (Washington, D.C.: U.S. Government Printing Office, 1969), p. ii.
26. J. Demos, "Female Role Orientation and Participation in a Woman's Voluntary Association," *Social Science,* 1975, Vol. 50, No. 3, pp. 136–40.
27. M.W. Mueller, "Economic Determinants of Volunteer Work by Women," *Signs,* 1975, Vol. 1, pp. 325–38. See also J. Jenner, "Participation, Leadership, and the Role of Volunteerism among Selected Women Volunteers," *Journal of Voluntary Action Research,* 1982, Vol. 11, No. 4, pp. 27–38.
28. D. Leat, "Explaining Volunteering: A Sociological Perspective," in J. Hatch, ed., *Volunteers: Patterns, Meanings, and Motives* (London, Great Britain: Cylinder Press, 1983), p. 55.
29. Secondary analysis of *Americans Volunteer–1974* data set by the author.
30. "Marching on Gallup," *AVA Update,* 1984, Vol. 23. No. 3, p. 1.
31. Gallup, op. cit., p. 12.
32. Cutler, 1977, op. cit.
33. P.K. Edwards, J.N. Edwards, and A.D. Watts, "Women, Work, and Social Participation," *Journal of Voluntary Action Research*, 1984, Vol. 13, No. 1, pp. 13, 16–17.
34. Chambré, 1985, op. cit., p. 295.
35. Kaye and Monk, op. cit. Newman et al., op cit.
36. G.G. Fillenbaum and G.L. Maddox, "Work after Retirement: An Investigation into Some Psychologically Relevant Variables," *The Gerontologist,* 1974, Vol. 14, pp. 418–24. See also Kaye and Monk, op cit.
37. Kaye and Monk, op. cit.
38. Edwards et. al., op. cit., p. 13.
39. Taietz and Larson, op. cit.
40. G.W. Domhoff, *The Higher Circles* (New York: Random House, 1970), pp. 34, 39–41. See also C. Slater, "Class Differences in Definition of Role and Membership in Voluntary Associations among Urban Married Women," *American Journal of Sociology,* 1960, Vol. 65, No. 6, pp. 616–19.
41. Schram and Dunsing, op cit., p. 379.
42. H. Hyman, op. cit.

43. P. Keith, 1980, op. cit., p. 71.
44. H. Hyman, op. cit.
45. Petrowsky, op. cit., pp. 752–53.
46. Wan and Odell, op. cit.
47. L.A. Morgan, "Continuity and Change in the Labor Force Activity of Recently Widowed Women," *The Gerontologist,* 1984, Vol. 24, No. 5, p. 533.

7

Race, Religion, and Volunteering among Older People

S
ince the experience of growing older has such a major impact on people's lives, it has traditionally overshadowed much of the diversity within the older population. Social gerontologists have focused on the common experiences of the aged and paid less attention to differences within this age group based on generational, racial, religious, ethnic, and social class differences within the older population. Compared to other areas of study (such as retirement), relatively little is known about religious, racial, and ethnic differences in the older population. This gap in the gerontological literature has been recognized since a good deal of excellent research is now being done on the special experiences and social service needs of older people in different racial and ethnic groups.[1]

At all ages, members of various religious and racial groups have different types and levels of involvement in a variety of social activities. The connections between race, religion, and volunteering have not been studied in detail and the amount of information on these subjects is very limited. Similarly, not much is known about religious and racial differences in volunteering by older people. This chapter looks at the effects of these two ascribed status characteristics and considers how they are related to volunteering in the older population.

Religion and Volunteering

Review of the Literature

Three dimensions of people's religious identity have been studied in detail. The first is religious affiliation: whether a person is Protestant, Catholic, or Jewish. A second area of concern is the level of religiosity. This has been measured in various ways, most often by finding out how often people attend religious services. Church or synagogue attendance is an imperfect measure but is the most widely used because it is possible to apply it to religions with different sets of practices. It is also not clear whether this is a measure of religious commitment or of social interaction occurring in the context of a religious institution.

A substantial amount of research has been done on the life-style differences between members of various religious groups; far less is known about some of these differences within the older population. One fairly well researched issue is the connection between religious affiliation and voluntary association membership. Most of the studies on this subject reach the conclusion that there are substantial differences between the three major religious groups. Protestants and Jews have significantly higher levels of participation than Catholics.[2] A more recent study, which was published in 1982, suggests that this difference is narrowing for Catholics and for Protestants.[3] These findings might reflect an historical change in which people in various religious groups behave similarly since the daily behavior of most Americans is more influenced by secular values than by religious values. For members of older generations, however, religious affiliation might still be meaningful since they grew up in a society where the role of religion in people's lives was probably far stronger than it is today.

There has also been some interest in the effect of religious involvement on older people's lives. Most often, this has been reflected in an interest in changes in religious commitment during old age rather than religious differences within the older population. Even though a good deal of older people's social participation takes place in the context of religious institutions,[4] church attendance appears to decline as people age.[5] However, a closer look suggests that this association is more complex. Church attendance declines for some people, remains stable for others, and increases for still others. When respondents in the Duke Longitudinal Survey were asked to estimate changes in their own frequency of church attendance, 45 percent said that they attended church less than at the age of 55. Close to one in five reported that they attended church more often; about four in ten attended church with a similar frequency.[6] Firmer conclusions on the effects of aging on religious attendance await reexamination in other longitudinal studies tracking changes in church attendance over time.

The Role of Volunteering in Different Faiths

Just as there are religious differences in patterns of voluntary association membership, so too should there be religious differences in patterns of volunteering. Far less empirical research has focused on the connection between religion and volunteering than on other factors. This is probably because the two *Americans Volunteer* studies, done in 1965 and 1974, were conducted by the U.S. Bureau of the Census, which does not collect data about religion. The 1981 Gallup survey included religious affiliation and found that Jews were far more involved in volunteering than others—64 percent of them did volunteer work. Half of the Protestants and 52 percent of the Catholics were volunteers.[7] These statistics are consistent with a study of the social relationships of Protestants and Catholics which found that differences between them were far narrower than in the past.[8]

Religious affiliation has a significant impact on older people's patterns of volunteering. There are sizeable differences between all three major religious groups. The highest frequency of participation, 32 percent, was for the Jews in the sample. One quarter of Protestants were volunteers and, consistent with studies of voluntary association membership, the lowest level of participation occurred among the Catholics. Only 17 percent of them were involved in doing volunteer work.

Taken together, the findings on voluntary association membership and volunteering suggest that religious affiliation continues to have a major impact on older people's patterns of social relationships. A recent study of Catholics and Protestants suggests, however, that these differences may become less pronounced in the future.[9]

Since all three religions stress the importance of "good deeds," the difference between levels of participation of members of these three groups merits further consideration. One possibility is that there are differences in the importance of religion in people's lives in the three groups. The crude but useful indicator of religiosity—church or synagogue attendance—was included in the interview and answers were coded into six categories ranging from "within the last day or two" to "never."

It is logical to assume that people who attend services more regularly would be more influenced by the importance of good works as a religious act. Regular attendance should be positively associated with volunteering. This did, in fact, occur. Seventy percent of volunteers attended church one or more times each week compared to half of the nonvolunteers. This relationship exists within each of the three major religious groups. Among Protestants, 71 percent of volunteers and 48 percent of nonvolunteers attended church weekly. For Catholics, 71 percent of volunteers and 57 percent of nonvolunteers went to church weekly. The number of Jewish respondents is relatively small—there were only 31 of them—but the same relationship appears; 30 percent of volunteers and 19 percent of nonvolunteers went to synagogue weekly.

One difference between the three groups that could account for the disparity between them in the proportion of volunteers is that they differ in the average educational level of their members. The Catholics were less educated as a group since 27 percent of the Protestants, 15 percent of the Catholics, and 52 percent of the Jews had attended college. The difference in volunteer participation between the three groups is partly due to differences in the educational levels of their members. However, even among the college-educated, a higher proportion of Protestants (43 percent) than Catholics (34 percent) were volunteers.

Several explanations have been offered for the lower involvement of Catholics in voluntary associations. Lenski's extensive study of the three major religious groups concluded that they differ in the relative strength of communal and religious ties. For Catholics, the religious ties are strong, but the communal ties are relatively weak. Among Jews, the religious ties are weaker than the ties to the Jewish community. Thus, for Catholics, the primary emphasis is their involvement in religious activities, while for Jews, the ties are to a community and to a people, and much less to a set of religious practices. Among Protestants, Lenski concluded that the ties to the two are fairly equal.[10]

A more satisfying explanation for differences between Protestants and Catholics is found in a study by Peterson and Lee, who looked at two groups, Catholics and Lutherans. They found higher church attendance among Catholics but higher involvement in church-related activities other than worship among the Lutherans, who also spent more time in voluntary associations that were secular in nature. To explain this, they speculated on the ways the religious obligations of the two groups influenced participation in voluntary associations and in church activities other than worship.

> The Catholic, fulfilling a specific obligation incurred by virtue of his religious affiliation through attendance at Sunday services, may feel that his duties are accomplished by this act and thus experience less pressure, both social and psychological, to participate in other church-sponsored activities. The religious duties of the Lutheran, on the other hand, are more diffuse. In the absence of a formal attendance requirement, the level of participation necessary to fulfill religious obligations is relatively undefined. This, perhaps, produces a tendency toward greater voluntary church participation.[11]

A second reason for differences in social participation is a result of differences between Catholic and Protestant churches as organizations. Authority is highly centralized in the Catholic church and the role of the laity in church governance is limited. Catholics have little experience in church-based participation. In contrast, the role of the laity is much greater in Protestant churches. "Participation in the activities of Protestant churches may provide training for members which facilitates participation in other voluntary associations."[12] This argument can also be used to explain the high level of involvement of Jews. For them, the main role of a rabbi is as a teacher. In congregations with a well-educated laity, services can be conducted with limited involvement by professional clergy.

Three differences between the major religions might account for the varying levels of volunteer participation by their members: the relative strengths of religious or communal ties, the nature of religious obligations, and the structure of authority within religious institutions. These, rather than differences in beliefs, account for higher levels of involvement by Protestants and Jews than by Catholics.

Race and Volunteering

Racial Differences in the Older Population

Relatively little is known about racial and ethnic differences in the older population, although this situation is being corrected because of the excellent research now being done on this topic. One would assume that life-style differences between racial groups continue into old age. It could also be possible that the aging process would narrow some differences between racial and ethnic groups since retirement has an income-leveling effect. Even though existing studies provide some important information about similarities and differences between racial and ethnic groups in the older population, there are still significant gaps in our knowledge.

A great deal of attention has been devoted to the relative economic status of blacks and whites. As is true at all age levels, a substantial percentage of older blacks are economically disadvantaged. Their position is also unfavorable when compared to older whites. Only a small percentage of older blacks are financially secure. In 1984, 11 percent of whites over the age of 65 were below the poverty level. Far more blacks and Hispanics were in this situation—close to one-third of older blacks and one-fifth of Hispanics were poor.[13] Since poverty and ill health are closely related, it is also quite understandable that another major difference between older blacks and older whites is that the former are generally in poorer health.[14]

Even though blacks face major financial problems in old age, there are other aspects of their lives that might make the experience of growing older less difficult for them than for whites. Blacks in general show more positive attitudes toward older people than whites.[15] Older blacks are also more socially integrated since they have more contact with neighbors, attend church more often,[16] and have more contact with relatives than do older whites.[17] Several recent studies suggest that the extended family support of older blacks and older whites may not be as different as was once the case and that there is considerable variation among blacks as to their levels of family contact in old age.[18]

Two major changes in old age, widowhood and retirement, may be experienced differently by blacks and by whites. A major study of widowhood found that more black women viewed widowhood to be problem-free (13 percent) than did white women (6 percent).[19] There are also differences in perceptions, attitudes, and experiences of blacks and whites with regard to retirement. The 1974 Harris survey included a series of questions on attitudes toward retirement. A special analysis of these data that looked at black–white differences showed that more older blacks looked forward to retirement (30 percent of blacks versus 17 percent of whites) and more often believed that people retire by choice (77 percent versus 69 percent for whites). Blacks probably adjust better to retirement since more of them look forward to retiring and once they leave the labor force, they miss work less than whites.[20]

There are also some differences between the two races in the ways they spend their leisure time. Older blacks more often spent time in passive and solitary activities—doing nothing, sitting and thinking, and sleeping. Blacks and whites were equally involved in many activities outside their homes such as going to movies, to senior centers, or to community centers.[21] Some of these findings might be due to class differences, but such an analysis has not been done. Only one study has actually considered the impact of socio-economic status on the activities of older blacks and older whites. It is based on 280 respondents interviewed in 1954 for the Duke Panel Study. When socioeconomic status was held constant, there was only a small difference between the activity levels of the two groups with one exception. Blacks had higher levels of religious involvement than whites of similar social status.[22] There are also sizeable class differences in the leisure activities selected by black retirees.[23]

Voluntary Association Membership among Blacks and Whites

There is a considerable amount of evidence that blacks have lower levels of voluntary association membership than whites. This finding could mean several things. It could reflect cultural differences between racial groups or could mainly be due to socioeconomic differences between the two groups. Blacks might belong to voluntary groups less than whites because they have lower incomes and less schooling as a group. In fact, the association between race and member-ship has been significantly modified when socioeconomic status has been con-trolled. Two different conclusions have been reached: that blacks either have fairly similar levels of participation as whites of equal status or that they have higher participation than whites at similar class levels.[24]

In addition to the levels of affiliation, there has been interest in whether blacks and whites belong to different types of organizations. Mainly, the focus has been on membership in religious or secular organizations. Blacks are more likely to belong to churches than whites, and much of their organizational in-volvement is in religious organizations.[25] This difference occurs when older blacks and older whites of similar status levels are compared.[26]

Black–white differences in levels and types of memberships in voluntary associations appear to continue into old age. When socioeconomic differences are considered, older blacks are either equally likely to be affiliated with volun-tary associations[27] or actually have higher membership levels.[28] A major reason, then, that participation of whites may be higher than blacks is because of class differences between the two racial groups.

Volunteering by Blacks and Whites: Previous Findings

Only one study of black–white differences in old age considers the subject of volunteering. It is based on the 1974 Harris survey and found that whites were more often engaged in doing volunteer work (23 percent) than blacks (18 percent). The major question on the subject of the behavior patterns of blacks and whites is whether they are due to life-style differences between the two groups or if they are essentially a reflection of the fact that blacks and whites are concentrated in different socioeconomic levels.

Volunteering by Older Blacks, Whites, and Hispanics:
Findings from the Harris Survey

There were a sufficient number of respondents to create three racial categories and one ethnic category for the sample: whites, blacks, members of other racial groups, and Hispanics. There are significant differences in the proportion of each group working as volunteers: 26 percent of whites, 17 percent of blacks, 13 percent of Hispanics, and 16 percent of members of other groups. This relationship is also statistically significant ($x^2 = 24.2$, $df = 3$, $p < .001$). Since several other studies of patterns of voluntary association membership found that racial differences diminished when socioeconomic status was controlled, I looked at whether or not this occurred with regard to volunteering.

Each of the indicators of socioeconomic status was introduced separately in table 7–1. The statistics show that black–white differences are, in fact, mainly due to socioeconomic differences. Blacks and whites who were high school graduates or who had less schooling were about equally involved in volunteering. Participation was slightly higher among blacks with some college or even more education (46 percent) than among whites with that much schooling (42 percent). Similarly, there are no substantial differences between the two major races in most of the occupational groups. Among professionals, blacks were more often engaged in volunteering than whites; half of the black and 42 percent of the white professionals were volunteers. However, in the job categories where blacks are most concentrated (unskilled blue collar jobs and service or farm jobs), they were less often volunteers (12 percent) than whites in such jobs (18 percent). When income differences are considered, the participation of blacks and whites is almost identical with one exception, the $10,000 to $14,999 group.

Socioeconomic differences do not completely explain the lower participation of Hispanics. Since Hispanics are concentrated in the groups with lower educational levels, and the number of Hispanics in higher income and job categories is small, it is difficult to make comparisons. Nonetheless, when compared with their black and white counterparts, Hispanics tend to be less actively involved in doing volunteer work. Relatively smaller proportions of well-educated Hispanics and those with high incomes are involved in volunteering.

Table 7–1

Percentage of Respondents Who Volunteer by Race and Ethnicity, Controlling for Indicators of Socioeconomic Status

Indicator of Socioeconomic Status	Race and Ethnicity					
	White		Black		Hispanic	
Educational achievement *(n = 2,038)*						
8 years or fewer	10	(206)	8	(134)	10	(125)
9 to 11 years	17	(530)	19	(100)	13	(46)
High school graduate	27	(345)	23	(39)	21	(24)
Some college or more	42	(450)	46	(28)	36	(11)
Current or former occupation *(n = 1,704)*						
Professional	42	(201)	50	(28)	*	(5)
Manager, proprietor, or sales	33	(284)	*	(5)	*	(8)
Clerical or skilled blue collar	23	(329)	29	(14)	32	(28)
Operative, service, or farm	18	(464)	12	(233)	10	(105)
Annual household income *(n = 1,729)*						
$6,999 or less	16	(452)	15	(171)	8	(110)
$7,000–$9,999	24	(221)	26	(43)	19	(36)
$10,000–$14,999	32	(241)	19	(32)	21	(19)
$15,000 or more	37	(369)	38	(21)	14	(14)

Note: Numbers in parentheses indicate number out of total sample who fall in that racial/ethnic and educational, occupational, or income category.

*Insufficient cases for calculation.

These findings are quite tentative, however, since the number of cases is very small. One explanation offered for the lower voluntary association membership of Puerto Ricans is cultural—their subculture may "discourage formal affiliation."[29] It is important to consider another reason for the lower participation of Hispanics—most of them are Catholic.

Within racial and ethnic categories, there might be substantial differences between men and women. A study conducted in New York found that lower class black women had especially high levels of membership in voluntary associations when they were compared with black men.[30] There were no significant gender differences either within or between the three major groups in this study population. Older black women were less often engaged in doing volunteer work (16 percent) than older white women (25 percent). Volunteering was slightly more common for black men (19 percent) than for black women. Occupational differences modified but did not reduce black–white differences among the women; black women were less often involved in doing volunteer work than white women in similar job categories. The only exception is among those in professional jobs. For these women, the likelihood of doing volunteer work was equal for the two groups.

Summary

There are significant differences in the levels of volunteer participation on the part of members of different religious groups and those with either different racial or ethnic identities. Protestants and Jews had a far greater tendency to volunteer than Catholics. This finding is quite consistent with earlier research on the association between religious affiliation and participation in voluntary associations. For all three groups, volunteering was positively associated with the frequency of church attendance. There are also significant differences between blacks, whites, and Hispanics. Whereas socioeconomic differences might account for the lower participation of blacks, this is not the case for Hispanics. Their lower involvement may mainly be a result of their being Catholic.

Notes

1. See four excellent articles on the special needs of Chinese, Korean, Puerto Rican, and black elderly in *The Gerontologist,* 1985, Vol. 25, No. 5.
2. B. Lazerwitz, "Membership in Voluntary Associations and Frequency of Church Attendance," *Journal of the Scientific Study of Religion,* 1962, Vol. 2, pp. 74–84. J.C. Peterson and G.R. Lee, "Religious Affiliation and Social Participation: Differences between Lutherans and Catholics," *Journal of Voluntary Action Research,* Vol. 5, No. 2, pp. 82–94.
3. W.A. McIntosh and J.P. Alston, "Lenski Revisited: The Linkage Role of Religion in Primary and Secondary Groups," *American Journal of Sociology,* 1982, Vol. 87, pp. 852–82.
4. D.O. Moberg, "Religiosity in Old Age," in B.L. Neugarten, ed., *Middle Age and Aging* (Chicago: University of Chicago Press, 1968), p. 500.
5. Ibid., p. 503. See also H.M. Bahr, "Aging and Religious Disaffiliation," *Social Forces,* 1970, Vol. 49, No. 1, pp. 59–71.
6. Palmore, op. cit., pp. 52–53.
7. Gallup, op. cit., p. 14.
8. McIntosh and Alston, op. cit.
9. Ibid.
10. G. Lenski, *The Religious Factor: A Sociologist's Inquiry* (Garden City, N.Y.: Doubleday, 1961), pp. 36–41.
11. J.C. Peterson and G.R. Lee, op. cit., p. 90.
12. Ibid., p. 91.
13. *Statistical Abstracts 1986,* Table 769.
14. M. Jackson and J.L. Wood, *Aging in America: Implications for the Black Aged* (Washington, D.C.: National Council on the Aging, 1976), pp. 28–29.

15. J.C. Register, "Aging and Race: A Black–White Comparative Analysis," *The Gerontologist,* 1981, Vol. 21, pp. 438–43.

16. Jackson and Wood, op. cit., p. 18.

17. See R.W. Kernodle and R.L. Kernodle, "A Comparison of the Social Networks of Black and White Elderly in a Southern Border State," paper presented at the Annual Meeting of the Gerontological Society, 1979, Washington, D.C.

18. Jackson and Wood, op. cit., pp. 16–18. See also R.J. Taylor, "The extended Family as a Source of Support to Elderly Blacks," *The Gerontologist,* 1985, Vol. 25, No. 5, pp. 488–95.

19. H. Lopata, op. cit., p. 72.

20. Jackson and Wood, op. cit., pp. 8–9, table 2.

21. Ibid., p. 20.

22. D.K. Heyman and F.C. Jeffers, "Study of the Relative Influences of Race and Socio-Economic Status Upon the Activities and Attitudes of a Southern Aged Population," *Journal of Gerontology,* 1970, Vol. 19, No. 2, p. 226.

23. M.L. Lambing, "Leisure Time Pursuits among Retired Blacks by Social Status," *The Gerontologist,* Vol. 12, pp. 363–67.

24. G. Anteenes and C.M. Gaitz, "Ethnicity and Participation: A Study of Mexican-Americans, Blacks and Whites," *American Journal of Sociology,* 1975, Vol. 80, pp. 1192–211. S.M. Cohen and R.E. Kapsis, "Participation of Blacks, Puerto Ricans and Whites in Voluntary Associations: A Test of Current Theories," *Social Forces,* 1978, Vol. 56, No. 4, pp. 1053–71. M. Oleson, "Social and Political Participation of Blacks," *American Sociological Review,* 1970, Vol. 35, pp. 682–97.

25. N. Babchuk and R. Thompson, "The Voluntary Associations of Negroes," *American Sociological Review,* 1962, Vol. 27, pp. 647–55. K.E. Davis, "Blacks and Voluntary Action: A Review of the Literature," *Voluntary Action Leadership,* Summer 1977, pp. 17–21.

26. Heyman and Jeffers, op. cit., p. 227.

27. Ibid., p. 226.

28. F. Clemente, P.A. Rexroad, and C. Hirsch, "The Participation of the Black Aged in Voluntary Associations," *The Journal of Gerontology,* 1975, Vol. 30, pp. 469–72.

29. S.M. Cohen and R.E. Kapsis, op. cit., p. 1066.

30. Ibid., p. 1062.

8
Older Volunteers as Joiners

One of this book's recurring themes has been that the people who would be expected to have more time to volunteer—homemakers and people who are completely retired—are less often involved in doing volunteer work than those who should have less time because they continue to work. This finding is partly due to age, health, and social status differences; when people of the same age, educational level, and occupation are compared, those who are completely retired have participation levels about equal to the semiretired.

It is important to think about these findings from another perspective: people with similar characteristics who are either homemakers or completely retired should be *more* frequently involved in doing volunteer work by virtue of the fact that they theoretically have more free time.

These findings redirected this book in a way not originally envisioned: to look at a broader set of questions concerning the place of volunteering in older people's lives. Volunteering appears to be part of a pattern of adjustment to old age which is less influenced by the objective amount of time people have than by their perception of leisure and the ways they choose to spend time.

This chapter focuses on volunteering in the context of people's other free-time activities. It looks at several issues. The first is the connection between volunteering and other activities. In this case, volunteering is used as an independent variable to see if volunteers and nonvolunteers have different leisure styles.

There is substantial evidence (see chapter 1) that a good deal of the free time gained with retirement is allocated to passive activities and to solitary ones. Time is a flexible rather than a fixed entity. The data suggest that an old saw is probably quite true: If you want something done, ask a busy person. The effect of retirement on this aspect of adjustment to old age is not clear-cut; an increase in the objective amount of leisure time people have does not, apparently, lead to higher involvement in many types of activities, including volunteering.

A second issue is whether or not people who are fully retired volunteer less often because they are generally less active. A third and final issue is whether volunteering is one aspect of a generally higher level of activity. If this is the case, the measure of activity would be an intervening variable between the characteristics already found to be related to volunteering. The introduction of the activity measure would reduce the associations between volunteering and the variables that influenced it, such as age, race, religion, and socioeconomic status.

Volunteering as Leisure and Unpaid Work

Volunteering has a diverse set of motivations and a number of different benefits, while it can be performed in several very different ways. It can serve as unpaid work, as one facet of membership in a voluntary association, or as a leisure activity. If it is viewed as work that receives no payment, then people would volunteer in order to strive toward specific goals or to gain the kind of personal satisfaction that comes from a job well done. Like paid work, volunteering fosters informal social interaction and can therefore be defined as a leisure activity. Since a good deal of volunteering occurs within the context of voluntary associations, it is probably closely linked to membership. Surprisingly, the connection between volunteering and voluntary association membership has not been systematically studied. As a leisure activity, volunteering can provide a person with a pleasurable set of experiences.

An important difference between the leisure activities and the volunteer activities of younger people and older people is that they occur in the context of different sets of obligations; the demands of work and family responsibilities are usually far less for older people. Leisure activities, voluntary association membership, and a good deal of volunteering are linked to other roles. For many women, it is an extension of being a mother since they commonly participate in organizations providing educational or recreational services to their children.

The motivations have traditionally been thought to be different for men. Even though men volunteer in ways connected to their family obligations (in scouting and little league), volunteering can be linked to their work. In some occupations and work settings, employees are expected to be involved in communal work; voluntary association membership can have a positive impact on a person's career by fostering social contacts that can become work-related acquaintances. Indeed, volunteer administrators view the workplace as the most efficient place to recruit men. As more and more women spend substantial portions of their lives in the labor force, they will also be in jobs where communal activities are expected and will volunteer for work-related reasons. For older people, then, the motivations for doing volunteer work change since work- and family-related volunteering are not as prevalent.

Older Volunteers as Joiners

Two studies of some of the ways that older volunteers were different from non-volunteers found that the most important distinction between them was the way they perceived and used their leisure time. Older volunteers were "joiners"; they were more actively involved in voluntary associations and had had a greater history of participation over the course of their lives. The nature of their participation in voluntary associations and leisure activities differed in several ways. Volunteers belonged to more organizations and gained more pleasure from their membership; a larger proportion of them viewed their involvements as enjoyable and meaningful. Another difference was that the volunteers were more inclined to spend time in goal-oriented activities rather than in informal social interaction with friends and family.[1]

One of these studies, which was based on a sample of people who attended a senior center, also found that the volunteers had less free time and easily found ways to fill up any free time they did have.[2]

Social and Leisure Activities in the Study Population

Each respondent was asked to indicate how frequently he or she was involved in fifteen different activities ranging from sitting and thinking to visiting friends and neighbors. The questions reflect an interest in understanding how often people spent time in various activities. This is a crude approach; a more precise method of studying allocation of leisure time is to ask people to keep a diary, the procedure used in time-budget studies.

There are several ways activities can differ from each other.[3] They can take place in different sorts of settings: at home, in an impersonal meeting place (a park or a store), or within an institution (a senior center or community center). Some activities bring people together; others are solitary in nature. Activities can also vary in the importance individuals attach to them. Watching television on a daily basis is probably less meaningful to most people than going to church every day. Another distinction is the purpose they serve in people's lives. Some activities are instrumental or task-oriented and are directed toward achieving specific individual or collective goals. Others are not goal-oriented but enhance a person's emotional state.

It is also possible that both instrumental and emotional benefits could be derived from one activity, or that the same action could be performed in rather different ways. What might appear to be a goal-oriented activity could be an opportunity to socialize with like-minded people. For one person, a trip to the library could be a way to obtain books. Yet, for another person, it could be a way to meet with neighbors and friends and be the basis for a regular routine which could structure a significant block of time.

Most of the questions were coded into six categories which ranged from "within the last day or two" to "never." Some of the questions were coded into three categories: "a lot," "some but not a lot," and "never." To permit comparison between all of the items and the construction of a total index of social activity, all of the measures were transformed into six-point measures. This was done by doubling the scores for the questions with three choices. A score close to six indicated that the person had done the activity within the past day or two; a five indicated involvement within the past week or two.

How Time Is Spent

Table 8–1 shows how often people spent time in a number of different ways. The items are arranged in rank order based on the mean for each of them. The table also indicates the percentage who had spent some time at each one within the past day or two. The most common ways to spend time were visitig neighbors and relatives and socializing with friends. This finding is consistent with a great deal of research pointing out that both neighbors and relatives are a central part of older people's support systems.[4]

The third most common way to spend time is to watch television. However, it is important to look at the mean score, which is higher than a number of other activities, but also to consider what it actually means: that 37 percent of the respondents watched television within the past day or two. Given the

Table 8–1
Rank Order of Social and Leisure Activities of Respondents in the Sample

Activity	Mean	Standard Deviation	% Doing Activity in Past Day or Two	Number of Cases
Visit neighbors and relatives	4.97	1.2	44	2,076
Socialize with friends[a]	4.35	1.5	37	2,084
Watch television[a]	4.23	1.6	32	2,084
Read[a]	4.17	1.6	37	2,077
Sit and think[a]	4.04	1.6	35	2,074
Go to restaurants	3.96	1.6	19	2,060
Listen to the radio[a]	3.81	1.6	27	2,081
Recreation and hobbies[a]	3.47	1.6	24	2,082
Walk or exercise[a]	3.47	1.6	24	2,084
Care for family members[a]	3.20	1.8	23	1,567
Do nothing[a]	3.03	1.5	14	2,046
Go to movies	2.12	.9	1	2,025
Go to the library	2.02	1.5	3	2,040
Go to community centers	2.01	1.5	5	2,050
Go to senior centers	1.95	1.5	5	1,874

[a]These items include three choices; the percentage indicated are the respondents who indicated that they did these things "a lot."

central place of television viewing in the lives of many people of all ages, this proportion is not especially high and is, in fact, much lower than informal visiting and socializing with neighbors, friends, and relatives.

Older people spent the least amount of time going to community centers or to senior centers. This is a very important finding since both of them have an important place in planning recreational activities for senior citizens. As part of their most important but diffuse goal, to increase the well-being of older people, these centers have also been used to achieve other more specific goals: to provide nutritional and health information and services. The low utilization of these facilities suggests the need to reconsider their place in older people's lives and to explore some reasons for low attendance.

Components of the Activity Index

Fifteen questions were combined into an activity index. The responses to the questions were combined and, in order to include as many cases as possible, respondents were assigned their average score for the other questions when they did not answer one or two questions. No score was calculated if a respondent did not answer more than two questions. The data analysis originally used four separate indices. The activities were easily grouped into four types of activities: informal social interaction, attendance at two sorts of formal activities (senior centers and community centers), involvement in various leisure activities, and passive or solitary activities. Even though the activities appeared to be distinctive from each other and represented several different types of pastimes, they were either used individually or combined into one index. This was done for methodological and substantive reasons. The use of four individual indices provided less information than individual items and was less efficient in the multiple regression analysis than one overall index.

The use of one index was also appropriate because all of the individual items were highly correlated with each other. Most of the correlations were positive ones, but there were several exceptions—watching television, listening to the radio, sitting and thinking, and doing nothing. All four of these are passive and/or solitary in nature and were negatively associated with the rest of the items. The scoring on these items was reversed for the activity index so that spending a great deal of time watching television was given same score as spending very little time in recreational activities or hobbies.

Social and Leisure Activities of Volunteers and Nonvolunteers

The comparison of volunteers and nonvolunteers uses three different types of statistics. The first are the means for each of the individual items. Second is the proportion of volunteers and nonvolunteers who had spent some time at each one within the past day or two. The third measure is the total activity index.

As shown in table 8–2, volunteers scored significantly higher than nonvolunteers on all of the individual measures, except for the passive and solitary activities. Clearly, the volunteers were more active in a variety of ways. Nonvolunteers spent significantly more time in three of the four passive and solitary activities—watching television, sitting and thinking, and doing nothing. In contrast, the nonvolunteers spent their time in informal social interaction visiting neighbors and relatives, watching television, or socializing with friends.

These findings are similar in some respects to two earlier studies of the leisure patterns of volunteers and nonvolunteers; both of them found that volunteers had less free time and were able to more easily find ways to spend their time. One difference, however, is that while earlier studies found that the volunteers spent less time socializing with friends, neighbors, and family, the older volunteers who were studied here more often spent time in informal social interaction with friends, neighbors, and family than did the nonvolunteers.

Another way to look at the place of various types of activities is to consider their relative rank for the volunteers and for the nonvolunteers. For both of them, the most frequent activity is visiting neighbors or relatives. In contrast, the second most common activity for the nonvolunteers is watching television.

Table 8–2
Social and Leisure Activities of Volunteers and Nonvolunteers

Activity	Volunteers			Nonvolunteers		
	Mean	Rank	% Doing Activity in Past Day or Two	Mean	Rank	% Doing Activity in Past Day or Two
Visit neighbors and relatives	5.4	1	53	4.8	1	41
Socialize with friends[a]	4.9	2	53	3.2	3	32
Watch television	4.0	6	27	4.3	2	33
Read[a]	4.6	3	47	4.0	5	34
Sit and think[a]	3.6	8	23	4.2	4	38
Go to restaurants	4.6	4	28	3.8	6	16
Listen to radio[a]	3.7	9	25	3.8	7	27
Recreation and hobbies[a]	4.3	5	42	3.2	10	19
Walk or exercise[a]	4.0	7	35	3.4	8	21
Care for family members[a]	3.6	10	27	3.3	9	22
Do nothing[a]	2.6	11	6	3.2	11	17
Go to movies	2.3	14	1	2.1	12	1
Go to the library	2.6	12	5	1.8	13	2
Go to community centers	2.5	13	10	1.9	14	3
Go to senior centers	2.2	15	7	1.9	15	4

[a]These items include three choices.

Volunteers ranked this sixth after socializing with friends, reading, going to restaurants, and spending time in recreational activities or hobbies.

Both types gave low rankings to attendance at senior centers or community centers. Only 7 percent of the volunteers and 4 percent of the nonvolunteers had gone to a senior center within the past week. The volunteers ranked community centers slightly higher than senior centers, and one in ten of them had gone to a community center within the past week.

A look at the pastimes of both groups is important for understanding where and how older people might be recruited for volunteer work. In addition, the assignment of people to tasks with a resemblance to the kinds of activities they prefer will not only expand the numbers of volunteers, but also increase the chances that people continue to participate.

The correlation between volunteering and the total measure of activity is high ($r = .35$). Older volunteers had significantly higher scores ($\bar{x} = 3.97$) than the nonvolunteers ($\bar{x} = 3.46, F = 304.9, p < .001$). Volunteering is probably one facet of a more active life-style; people who choose to do "good deeds" when they are older are not only joiners—people more involved in voluntary associations[5]—but they have stronger connections to the society in a number of different ways. They are more involved in caring for other family members, go to restaurants more often, spend more time in recreational activities and hobbies, read more, and even socialize more with friends, neighbors, and relatives. In contrast, the nonvolunteers spend relatively more time in a variety of passive and solitary pursuits—watching television, sitting and thinking, and doing nothing.

In sum, older people who are involved in doing volunteer work are more active in all different types of social and leisure activities ranging from informal contact with friends, relatives, and neighbors, to going to the movies and to restaurants on a more frequent basis.

Activity Levels of Workers, Retirees, and Homemakers

There is a considerable amount of evidence—evidence discussed throughout this book but in special detail in the first chapter—that the increased amount of discretionary time resulting from retirement does not lead to more time spent in active leisure. What people appear to do, instead, is spend more time doing things that are passive in nature and that do not necessarily bring them into contact with other people.

This issue is, by itself, worthy of a complete book. Since these data suggest that volunteering is part of a leisure style that some older (and perhaps younger) people adopt, it is worthwhile to consider the connection between activity levels, employment status, and volunteer status. Indeed, the people who were working (either full-time or part-time) and those who were semiretired had about the same activity levels ($\overline{x}$ = 3.7). Those who were not working, either because they were homemakers or were fully retired, also had about the same activity levels as each other, $\overline{x}$ = 3.5, and these were significantly lower than for the older people who were working. The connection between high activity and volunteering is a strong one. After considering several factors that might have accounted for this relationship (such as the facts that the more active people were better educated, younger, in better health, and more affluent), the connection between volunteering and activity still remained strong.[6]

Therefore, work and leisure appear to reinforce each other rather than be mutually exclusive. This is part of a more general pattern in which older people with high levels of activity are also people who tend to continue to be working.

Perceived Health and Activity Levels of Volunteers and Nonvolunteers

Declining health can impose restrictions on older people's choice of activities. Even though the measure of health status used here (perceived health) may be an accurate gauge of people's physical capacity, it is also important to consider that health limitations could be interpreted differently by volunteers and by nonvolunteers. In fact, previous studies have shown that volunteers and nonvolunteers have similar levels of health and, in one study, volunteers had some impairments that should have limited their participation, but did not. A study based on samples drawn from three settings (residents of a housing project for the elderly, members of a senior center, and patients at a Veterans Administration clinic) found that there were many ways in which the volunteers and the nonvolunteers in these three groups were equally healthy. However, the volunteers more often had hearing or visual problems.[7] In fact, volunteers are a more active group regardless of their health. The highest activity scores were for the volunteers who were in excellent health ($\overline{x}$ = 4.0) and the least active were the nonvolunteers in poor health ($\overline{x}$ = 3.1). However, when volunteers were compared with nonvolunteers in similar health, the former were appreciably more active. For example, volunteers in excellent health had an average activity score of 4.0 while the nonvolunteers had a lower score of 3.7. Indeed, the volunteers in poor health were slightly more active ($\overline{x}$ = 3.8) than the nonvolunteers in excellent health.

Older Volunteers as Joiners

Volunteering is one facet of a more general style of higher social participation by many older adults. This observation has been implied in several earlier studies but not actually tested in a systematic way. It is possible to look at whether or not volunteering is one facet of a more active life-style by seeing if the various social and demographic characteristics that predispose people to volunteer actually continue to influence it when a person's activity level is held constant. This was done (as seen in table 8–3) by creating two multiple regression analyses.

The first included all of the variables associated with volunteering. (See the appendix for a description of these variables and how they were coded for the regression analysis.) The second model included all of the same variables and the activity index as well. The results show that the model including activity has a higher R^2, which means that the variables contained in it explain more of the variance (15.5 percent) in volunteer status than in the model that does not include ACTIVITY (where the $R^2 = .108$), which explains about 11 percent of the variance. In fact, ACTIVITY alone explained 13 percent of the variance. Several of the demographic and social characteristics that originally influenced volunteering (perceived health, income, religion, and occupation) probably affect volunteering indirectly and have a greater impact on ACTIVITY instead. Education and age, on the other hand, have a strong effect on volunteering which is independent of their influence on ACTIVITY.

Volunteering is one facet of a more active life-style in old age which is, in turn, more common for those segments of the older population that are younger, better educated, and in better health. Even though there are some differences, neither volunteering nor high activity are directly influenced by role-loss variables: employment status, marital status, being widowed, work deprivation, and living alone. Other social characteristics (such as income, religion,

Table 8–3
Results of Stepwise Multiple Regression Analysis Predicting Volunteer Status
(standardized beta weights)

Variable	Model 1: Demographic Characteristics and Perceived Health	Model 2: Demographic Characteristics, Perceived Health, and Activity
EDUCATION	.143	.112
PERHEALTH	.102	n.s.
AGE	−.097	−.079
INCOME	.064	n.s.
RELIGION	.066	n.s.
OCCUPATION	.078	.072
GENDER	n.s.	n.s.
RACE	n.s.	n.s.
ACTIVITY		.278
Adjusted R^2	.108	.155

n.s. = not significant.

and occupation) have an impact on volunteering, but they are more minor influences compared to education and activity.

Summary

Volunteering is one aspect of a more active life-style during old age. Older volunteers were more often involved in a whole range of social and leisure pursuits; in contrast, the nonvolunteers spent relatively more time in passive and solitary activities. These are part of a larger set of ways some people adjust to old age. Total retirement from work is associated with a lower activity level, regardless of a person's health, education, or income. Volunteers are less affected by declining health since, even when their health is poor, they spend more time in a variety of social and leisure activities.

Social gerontologists have been especially interested in looking at whether or not high levels of social involvement have a positive impact on the well-being of the elderly. Volunteering, in particular, has been designed as a way to increase older people's well-being since it is viewed as a meaningful way older people can spend their time. The existence and nature of the association between volunteering and life satisfaction is the subject of the next chapter.

Notes

1. Dye et al., op. cit., p. 217. Mellinger and Holt, op. cit., p. 456.
2. Dye et al., op. cit., p. 218.
3. C.N. Bull, "Leisure Activities," in D.J. Mangen and W.A. Peterson, eds., *Research Instruments in Social Gerontology: Social Roles and Social Participation* (Minneapolis: University of Minnesota Press, 1982), pp. 500–5.
4. See M. Cantor, "The Formal and Informal Social Support System of Older New Yorkers," paper presented at the International Congress of Gerontology, 1975.
5. For a description of the term *joiner*, see M. Hauskenecht, *The Joiners* (New York: Bedminster Press, 1962).
6. When the correlation between volunteer status and activity was recalculated and a number of controls were introduced, the relationship continued to exist. For example, when age and perceived health were introduced, the correlation between activity and volunteering was .30. The introduction of the three indicators of socioeconomic status (education, income, and occupation) resulted in a correlation of $r = .27$.
7. Hunter and Linn, op. cit., p. 209.

9
Does Volunteering Improve Life Satisfaction?

Americans strive to achieve happiness and expect to be happy—a quest made possible by the high level of financial security in this society. The position of older people is a unique one. Even though they are disproportionately among the economically disadvantaged, most of them are economically secure and, at the same time, they have been freed from many of the daily responsibilities confronting younger people. This "freedom" is not always a source of liberation. This added time can weigh heavily on some people's hands.

In the context of a society where older people are a leisure class, the issue of life satisfaction gains special meaning. The first chapter described the challenge to older people—and to those who plan and conduct programs for them—to structure meaningful lives in the absence of substantial work and family obligations. A good deal of research has been devoted to identifying the factors that make a positive contribution to people's life satisfaction. These efforts have had a very practical impact on planning social programs for older people.

One of the most often discussed predictors of life satisfaction is social activity. High levels of participation in various social and leisure activities have a positive effect on adjustment to old age. An implicit assumption in planning programs for older people has been that they are happier when they are more active. This is based on activity theory, a viewpoint suggesting that older people will fare better when they are involved in a variety of social and leisure pursuits that substitute for roles that are "lost" as a result of retirement, widowhood, and changes in social networks as friends move or die. This theory has had a very clear impact on social policies and programs for older people. A number of different programs—senior centers, nutrition programs, and also programs to expand volunteering by older people—are designed to improve older people's levels of well-being by helping them to be more active.

Volunteering has been identified as one way to help older people to acquire meaningful social roles; it enables them to be altruistic, to gain new skills, and to become part of a social network of other volunteers. Another important benefit is that it places older people in intergenerational relationships, often as the donors of services to people younger—or older—than themselves. These intergenerational relationships are in themselves potentially beneficial in a society where age segregation is quite common.

This chapter considers whether there is a relationship between volunteering and life satisfaction. As one type of meaningful activity, involvement in volunteer work is viewed as having a positive impact on an older person's outlook. The chapter will look at the relationship between volunteering and life satisfaction and will consider two related criticisms of this research: first, that older people who are more active might be a self-selected group composed of people who initially have higher levels of life satisfaction; and second, that the impact of activity on life satisfaction is difficult to identify since the direction of the causality between them is difficult to establish. It is not clear whether volunteering has a positive impact on life satisfaction or if volunteers are a self-selected group composed of people with initially higher levels of life satisfaction.

Activity and Life Satisfaction

There is considerable support for a basic premise of activity theory, that there is a positive relationship between involvement in different social roles, levels of social activity, and life satisfaction.[1] Involvement in social and in leisure activities also appears to become more important as people grow older. Tobin and Neugarten found a stronger connection between activity and life satisfaction for people in their seventies than for people in their fifties or sixties.[2]

The presumed impact of activity on well-being has been subject to a good deal of criticism. Although the questions raised are quite diverse, all of them share a concern that an emphasis on the number of activities or the number of roles occupied greatly oversimplifies the actual sources of well-being. It is important to review some of these criticisms since they are pertinent to developing an understanding of how volunteering might contribute to older people's well-being.

Number, Types, and Meaning of Activities

In order to more carefully look at the relationship between life satisfaction and activity, it is necessary to make some distinctions between the various dimensions of social participation, namely, the number, types, and meaning of them, since not all activities have the same impact on people's well-being. A positive relationship exists between the number of different activities, the frequency of being involved in them, and life satisfaction.[3] In contrast, a recent study based on the 1974 Harris survey found that the number of leisure activities did not influence life satisfaction.[4] Not all activities had the same impact for residents of several retirement communities. Informal activities affected well-being much more than formal activities.[5] Contact with friends rather than with relatives or with neighbors had a more positive impact on life satisfaction.[6] Solitary activities—the kinds of activities men tend to spend more time doing when they retire—have no effect on life satisfaction.[7]

An understanding of why a high activity level could positively affect life satisfaction requires some attention to a whole other set of issues, most of which have received relatively little attention. People's perception of whether they are satisfied with their leisure may be much more important than the actual number of things they do or how often they do them. The sense of well-being may be more affected by spending time in ways viewed to be meaningful.[8] Life satisfaction may be higher when people are satisfied with their activity levels[9] and the amount of interaction and companionship they have[10] rather than being determined by a precise number of activities or social roles.

Models of Life Satisfaction

A different approach is to use multiple regression analysis to predict life satisfaction. Several types of independent variables have been used: measures of socioeconomic status, social integration, self-concept, health status, and personality. Two studies provide confirmation of the important impact of activity on life satisfaction. In one, activity was the strongest predictor of life satisfaction for men as well as for women.[11] Another model provided some additional reasons why activity enhanced life satisfaction. It showed that there were two intervening variables, social adequacy and self-conception. High activity enhances people's sense of well-being because activity has a positive effect on people's feelings about themselves which, in turn, are beneficial for their overall sense of well-being.[12]

Personality Factors and Life Satisfaction

Another viewpoint is that life satisfaction is a stable attribute of a person which is more influenced by personality than by a person's immediate social circumstances, such as how "busy" he or she is at the present time.[13] When personality (as measured by the Minnesota Multiphasic Personality Inventory) and activity measures were both included as predictors, personality was a more important influence, while a person's level of social interaction had no impact on well-being. The strongest predictor of life satisfaction, however, was a person's physical health.[14] Another study, based on the Duke Longitudinal Survey, identified the factors that predicted activity and life satisfaction. Two regression analyses were run, their results being quite different. Activity was mainly influenced by education, age, occupation, and employment status; life satisfaction was most influenced by personality. Since "psychological well-being and activity were best predicted by different personality and social status factors," the study reached the conclusion that their association is probably not as strong as it is usually assumed to be.[15]

Self-Selectivity and Activity

Several researchers have come to the conclusion that the association between life satisfaction and activity is spurious: the two appear closely related but, on further examination, the association between them is mainly due to the fact that they are essentially consequences of the same independent variables. Two studies, based on relatively small samples in Oberlin, Ohio, and in Kansas City, both found that the original correlations between life satisfaction and voluntary association participation did not exist when two important predictors of life satisfaction—health status and socioeconomic status—were held constant.[16] Higher life satisfaction looked as if it was associated with voluntary association membership because healthier and better-educated people tended to be more active in voluntary associations. Better-educated and healthier people were also happier. This led Cutler to observe, "voluntary associations self-select as members and as participants persons who are initially more satisfied with their life situation by virtue of their health and status characteristics."[17]

Since activities have a different impact on life satisfaction, the conclusion that the association between life satisfaction and activity is spurious should consider a number of other aspects of social activities. The impact of several types of social interaction were considered in a study of 323 respondents who were members of several different organizations, were clients of several social service agencies, or were recipients of government aid. Initially, there were strong relationships between well-being and a number of indicators of participation: the number of memberships, frequency of attendance, being in a leadership role, and how actively people participated. The introduction of socioeconomic status and health controls essentially eliminated these relationships.[18]

In contrast, two other studies came to very different conclusions. Both found that high levels of activity were positively associated with well-being even when health and socioeconomic status were taken into account.[19]

Questions Raised by Studies of Activity
and Life Satisfaction

All of these findings raise some serious questions about the effects of activity on life satisfaction. Some doubt has been cast on the connection between activity and life satisfaction since socioeconomic status, health, and personality may be far more important influences on life satisfaction than activity. This brief literature review suggests that the relationship between activity and life satisfaction is an important one with significant implications for theories of aging and for social policies directed at improving adjustment to old age. It is quite clear that there is a connection between activity and well-being that merits consideration. However, it is also important to continue to investigate the nature of that relationship by looking at the various dimensions of well-being, the types of factors that may be important intervening variables, and if activity influences life satisfaction or if people who are more active in old age are a self-selected group composed of individuals whose initially higher level of life satisfaction is an important precondition for their being more active.

Volunteering and Life Satisfaction

Volunteering has been viewed as an important way to improve older people's sense of well-being. Programs have been especially designed to increase their participation since it can be a meaningful way to spend time. However, a number of studies cast doubt on whether volunteering actually has this effect.

Several studies have found that there is a strong association between being a volunteer and having a higher level of life satisfaction. A group of volunteers at a Veterans Administration hospital in Miami were compared with several groups of nonvolunteers (clinic patients, senior center members, and residents of a senior citizen's housing complex). The volunteers were happier and better adjusted in several ways: they showed more will to live, had higher life satisfaction, reported fewer physiological symptoms of anxiety such as nervousness and shakiness, and presented less evidence of depression. These differences continued to exist even when social class and health status were held constant.[20] A second study, based on close to four hundred Western Canadians, looked at the connection between volunteering and life satisfaction in a very different way. Volunteer status was one variable used in a multiple regression analysis to predict life satisfaction. It was the second most important influence, next to education.[21] The results must be considered cautiously since the most important predictor of life satisfaction, health status, was not included in the analysis.

Only one other comparable study has looked at the association between life satisfaction and volunteering in a large, representative sample. It was based on the 1974 Harris survey which used a different measure of life satisfaction but many similar questions about activity. When other variables were held constant, there was no relationship between activity and life satisfaction.[22]

It is important not only that volunteering be associated with life satisfaction but that it actually improve it. The ideal way to test improvement is to measure life satisfaction of a group of people before they begin to volunteer and then again after a reasonable time interval. One way to approximate this has been to compare people who have actually volunteered with people who have applied for participation in a program. One study using this approach found that there were significantly higher levels of life satisfaction among participants in the Senior Companion Program than among people who had only applied to participate in it.[23]

Two further questions are whether volunteering has a greater effect on life satisfaction than other forms of social participation, and if it has a comparable impact on life satisfaction as work. It is not clear that volunteering has an especially great effect on life satisfaction.[24] Among senior center members, similar levels of well-being were expressed by volunteers and nonvolunteers.[25] It probably does not serve as a substitute for work in the sense that the levels of happiness and self-concepts of volunteers were lower than paid workers'.[26] Not all volunteer experiences are comparable. It is valuable to examine whether certain experiences are more beneficial than others and if the amount of time people spend as volunteers also makes a difference in the effect of the experience on life satisfaction. When Foster Grandparent and Senior Companion participants were compared with nonvolunteers on the waiting lists for the two programs, participation had no apparent effect on life satisfaction. However, when a different dependent variable was used, number of hours a week spent as a volunteer, there was a relationship. Volunteers who spent more time had higher levels of life satisfaction.[27]

The inconsistent results on the relationship between life satisfaction and volunteering should be considered in light of the findings of a study of volunteers, workers, and meal site participants. Not all volunteer work had the same impact. Some segments of the older population apparently derived a greater benefit from volunteering than other types of people; volunteering had an especially great impact on older people when they lived in cities, lived alone, or were in poor health. Participation in programs specifically designed for older people, such as the RSVP (Retired Senior Volunteer Program), was more effective than other types of volunteering.[28]

What Is Life Satisfaction?

The Harris survey included eighteen items measuring life satisfaction. When combined, they are a commonly used measure, the LSIA index. The survey includes a series of questions measuring four dimensions: whether or not the person derives pleasure from his or her everyday activities, whether a person has a sense of being responsible for the events in his life, if there is a congruence between the goals a person wanted and the goals achieved, and whether a person has a happy and optimistic mood tone. An important goal of the index was to create a measure that did not impose a judgment on the best way to adjust to the process of growing older; this was to measure levels of adjustment to old age from the individual's own viewpoint.[29]

Life satisfaction scores were computed for 2,085 of the respondents in this survey. Agreement with items indicating a positive outlook was given a score of 1 for each item; disagreement resulted in a score of 0 for each item. All eighteen items were combined so that the highest possible score would be 18. The mean score was 10.94 for the respondents; the standard deviation was 4.22.

Life Satisfaction of Volunteers and Nonvolunteers

There is a positive correlation ($r = .23$) between volunteering and life satisfaction. Volunteers had higher scores on this measure of well-being ($\bar{x} = 12.73$) than nonvolunteers ($\bar{x} = 10.41$, $F = 117.9$, $p < .001$).

As is the case in other studies on activity, the correlation between life satisfaction and volunteering could mainly be due to the fact that the volunteers are a self-selected group and would be expected to adapt better to old age since they are the better-educated, more affluent, and also younger segment of the older population. The association between volunteer status and life satisfaction might be spurious since the volunteers would already be a more satisfied group. This was the case in a study which used the 1974 Harris survey.[30]

There is a positive correlation between life satisfaction and being in better health ($r = .50$), being younger ($r = .10$), and three measures of socioeconomic status: education ($r = .32$), occupation ($r = .25$), and income ($r = .34$). Various measures of retirement (such as whether or not it was voluntary and retirement age) were not associated with life satisfaction, but two measures of family status—being widowed ($r = -.17$) and living alone, ($r = -.12$)— were negatively associated with life satisfaction.

Volunteering is significantly associated with life satisfaction even when other potentially confounding factors are considered. The partial correlation coefficients are reduced when other factors are taken into account, but the associations nonetheless remain significant. When age and perceived health are introduced, the partial correlation coefficient is $r = .15$. When the three measures of socioeconomic status are included, the partial correlation between volunteering and life satisfaction was $r = .15$.

These associations might not be the result of volunteering itself but, more likely, a result of high activity generally since older volunteers are more active. Therefore, the associations are part of the association between activity and life satisfaction. There is a high correlation between activity and life satisfaction ($r = .39$)—a much stronger association than between volunteering and life satisfaction. Unlike some previous studies, the association between the activity measure used here and life satisfaction is a strong one which is reduced but far from eliminated by introducing such significant determinants of both activity and life satisfaction as age and perceived health ($r = .24$), indicators of socioeconomic status ($r = .28$), and indicators of work status or limited family involvement ($r = .38$ when either widowhood or living alone are controlled or when employment status is controlled).

These data indicate that the strong connection between volunteering and life satisfaction occurs because volunteering is part of a high level of activity and, in and of itself, may not necessarily contribute more to an individual level of life satisfaction than high activity itself. In fact, when a multiple regression analysis was performed on predictors of life satisfaction (see table 9–1), volunteering was not a significant predictor of life satisfaction. Activity, on the other hand, was the second most important predictor of life satisfaction, next to health. In fact, activity level had a stronger impact on life satisfaction than the various measures of socioeconomic status.

Unravelling the Causality between
Activity and Life Satisfaction

The relationship between life satisfaction and activity is a central one in social gerontology and has important implications for understanding volunteering. The research that reaches the conclusion that voluntary groups select people with higher life satisfaction suggests that the causality might operate in the opposite direction, that people with higher levels of life satisfaction might be more active. In a summary of findings of the Duke Longitudinal Studies, Palmore suggested that an even more complex relationship might exist: "that there is mutual interaction such that health and activity contribute to life satisfaction and life satisfaction in turn contributes to health and activity."[31] This is an intriguing but as yet unexamined question since none of the studies of activity and life satisfaction have actually looked at whether people with higher levels of life satisfaction more often become more active[32] and if activity then positively affects life satisfaction.

Table 9–1
Results of Stepwise Multiple Regression Analysis
Predicting Life Satisfaction
(standardized beta weights)

Variable	With Activity	Without Activity
PERHEALTH	.345	.398
ACTIVITY	.186	
EDUCATION	n.s.	.102
INCOME	.096	.098
MARR	.096	.098
NWORK	−.088	−.069
RELIGION	.055	.053
OCCUPATION	.051	n.s.
NOWVOL	n.s.	n.s.
WIDOW	n.s.	n.s.
ALONE	n.s.	n.s.
GENDER	n.s.	n.s.
WHITE	n.s.	n.s.
Adjusted R^2	.332	.304

n.s. = not significant.

There are several ways to identify which of two variables might be the causal factor in a relationship. The first is temporal. If one variable precedes another in time, then it is likely that that one is the causal factor. Another criteria could be called "mutability." If one variable is more resistant to change, then it is more likely to be the causal factor. It is possible to argue that activity and life satisfaction are both subject to external influences. However, a number of researchers suggest that high activity is probably a stable characteristic, a finding that provides support for continuity theory.[33] Several researchers have also pointed out that life satisfaction is fairly stable over the course of a person's life[34] and is also influenced by one's parents' level of life satisfaction.[35]

Causality can also be determined by statistical measures. The use of multiple regression suggested that life satisfaction might influence activity since a regression equation predicting activity that included life satisfaction yielded a slightly higher beta weight for life satisfaction as predictor of activity ($b = .21$) than for activity as a predictor of life satisfaction ($b = .19$).

A different type of statistical analysis, LISREL, was undertaken in order to unravel the question of whether life satisfaction influences activity, if activity influences life satisfaction, or if life satisfaction influences activity. The results of the LISREL program resulted in a higher gamma coefficient (the coefficient of determination between two variables in a model that are both internal to the model) for life satisfaction than for activity. When activity was used to predict life satisfaction, the gamma for activity was $-.06$ while the gamma for life satisfaction as a predictor of activity was much higher, $.27$.

This confirms one criticism of the association between activity and life satisfaction, that people with high activity levels are initially a happier group. It is also possible that voluntary associations and possibly organizations that employ volunteers self-select those people who initially have higher levels of life satisfaction.

Summary

There is a strong relationship between volunteering and life satisfaction. This relationship exists even when factors such as age, perceived health, and socioeconomic status are held constant. Volunteering is not a predictor of life satisfaction, but is related to it because volunteering is one facet of a higher activity level. LISREL was used in order to unravel the direction of the causality between activity and life satisfaction. Its results show that high activity is a consequence, not a cause, of high levels of life satisfaction. Several directions for future research are also suggested. It is not only important to look at the association between volunteering and life satisfaction, as was done here, but also to look at the nature of volunteer experiences that do or do not contribute to higher levels of well-being: the nature of the volunteer job, whether or not the volunteering occurs as part of a specific program for older people, the conditions of the situation, and the amount of time spent doing volunteer work.

Notes

1. For a list of studies published before 1980, see N. Lohmann, "Life Satisfaction Research in Aging: Implications for Policy Development," in N. Datan and N. Lohmann, eds., *Transitions of Aging* (New York: Academic Press, 1980), p. 34.

2. S. Tobin and B. Neugarten, "Life Satisfaction and Social Interaction in the Aging," *Journal of Gerontology,* 1981, Vol. 16, p. 346.

3. R.A. Ward, "The Meaning of Voluntary Association Participation to Older People," *Journal of Gerontology,* 1974, Vol. 34, p. 440.

4. See J.R. Kelly, "Leisure in Later Life: Roles and Identities," in N.J. Osgood, op. cit.

5. C.F. Longino and C.S. Kart, "Explicating Activity Theory: A Formal Replication," *Journal of Gerontology,* 1982, Vol. 37, pp. 713–22.

6. B.W. Lemon, V.L. Bengtson, and J.A. Peterson, "An Exploration of the Activity Theory of Aging: Activity Types and Life Satisfaction Among In-Movers to a Retirement Community," *Journal of Gerontology,* 1972, Vol. 27, pp. 511–23.

7. Ibid. See also Longino and Kart, op. cit.

8. G.H. Maguire, "An Exploratory Study of the Relationship of Valued Activities to the Life Satisfaction of Elderly Persons," *The Occupational Therapy Journal of Research,* 1983, Vol. 3, No. 3, p. 170.

9. J.A. Mancini, "Leisure Satisfaction and Psychologic Well—Being in Old Age: Effects of Health and Income," *Journal of the American Geriatrics Society,* 1978, Vol. 26, p. 551.

10. M. Baldassare, S. Rosenfield, and K. Rook, "The Types of Social Relations Predicting Elderly Well-Being," *Research on Aging,* 1984, Vol. 6, p. 557.

11. K.S. Markides and H.W. Martin, "A Causal Model of Life Satisfaction among the Elderly," *Journal of Gerontology,* 1979, Vol. 34, No. 1, p. 89.

12. K.A. McClelland, "Self-Conception and Life Satisfaction: Integrating Aged Subculture and Activity Theory," *Journal of Gerontology,* 1982, Vol. 37, pp. 723–32.

13. See E. Palmore and V. Kivett, "Change in Life Satisfaction: A Longitudinal Study of Persons Aged 46–70," *Journal of Gerontology,* 1977, Vol. 32, No. 3, pp. 311–16; and P. Mussen, M. Honzik, and D. Eichorn, "Early Adult Antecedents of Life Satisfaction at Age 70," *Journal of Gerontology,* 1982, Vol. 37, No. 3, pp. 317–22.

14. G. Deimling and Z. Harel, "Social Integration and Mental Health of the Aged," *Research on Aging,* Vol. 6, No. 4, pp. 515–27.

15. L.K. George, "The Impact of Personality and Social Status Factors upon Levels of Activity and Psychological Well-Being," *Journal of Gerontology,* 1978, Vol. 33, No. 6, pp. 844–46.

16. S. Cutler, "Voluntary Association Participation and Life Satisfaction: A Cautionary Research Note," *Journal of Gerontology,* 1973, Vol. 28, No. 1, pp. 96–100. C.N. Bull and J.B. Aucoin, "Voluntary Association Participation and Life Satisfaction: A Replication Note," *Journal of Gerontology,* 1975, Vol. 30, No. 1, pp. 73–76.

17. Cutler, ibid., p. 99.

18. R.A. Ward, "The Meaning of Voluntary Association Participation to Older People," *Journal of Gerontology*, 1979, Vol. 34, No. 3, pp. 438–45.

19. Baldassare et al., op. cit., p. 556; and Mancini, op. cit., pp. 550–52.

20. Hunter and Linn, op. cit., pp. 209–11.

21. J. Bond, "Volunteerism and Life Satisfaction among Older Adults," *Canadian Counsellor*, 1982, Vol. 16, No. 3, pp. 168–72.

22. F. McLaughlin, "Volunteerism and Life Satisfaction in Older People," *The Gerontologist*, 1983, Vol. 23, p. 69.

23. C.J. Fogelman, "Being a Volunteer: Some Effects on Older People," *Generations*, 1981, Vol. 5, No. 4, pp. 24–25, 49.

24. Ward, op. cit., p. 440.

25. Dye et al., op. cit., p. 217.

26. Carp, op. cit., p. 499.

27. J.T. Rouse, *Life Satisfaction of the Elderly as Volunteer Social Support Providers*, Ph.D. dissertation, The Wright Institute, Berkeley, Calif., 1982.

28. A.P. Fengler, "Life Satisfaction of Subpopulations of Elderly: The Comparative Effects of Volunteerism, Employment, and Meal Site Participation," *Research on Aging*, 1984, Vol. 6, No. 2, p. 208.

29. Neugarten, Havighurst, and Tobin, 1961, p. 134.

30. McLaughlin, op. cit.

31. Palmore, op. cit., pp. 105–6.

32. Bull and Aucoin, op. cit., p. 76.

33. Ward, op. cit., p. 444.

34. Palmore and Kivett, op. cit., Palmore, op. cit., pp. 97–99.

35. Mussen, Honzik, and Eichorn, op. cit.

10
Volunteering, Activity, and Life Satisfaction: A Path Model of Volunteer Participation

A good deal of research has been devoted to identifying individual factors that are positively related to involvement in doing volunteer work; this book has confirmed most earlier findings. This chapter presents a model of volunteering that shows, both visually and statistically, how all of the factors influence volunteering and how they are in turn related to each other. Since the model only includes relationships that are significant, some of the important findings are not illustrated in the model. The discussion will describe the model and review some significant findings that are not illustrated in it.

The ISSTAL Model

There is one precedent for this effort, the ISSTAL model created by Smith.[1] This model includes a diverse set of variables (contextual elements, demographic characteristics, personality and intellectual abilities, attitudes, values and beliefs, and situational factors), all of which affect "discretionary" behavior. There are several important limitations of the ISSTAL model. First, a very broad range of behaviors are combined in the dependent variable. The term *discretionary behavior* includes a whole host of activities usually subsumed under the terms *leisure, informal social interaction, voluntary association membership*, and *volunteering*. It is not clear whether this broad range of behaviors should be combined in this manner. Very little is known about the connection between two areas of activity that are even as similar as volunteering and voluntary association membership, and even less is known about the relationships between all four of them.

Even though the individual relationships in the ISSTAL model are based on a vast range of empirical data, the entire model has never been tested with one set of data. While extremely useful for analytical purposes, it does not provide any sense of the relative importance of the influences of all of the variables. A third limitation is that the interrelationships among the variables are not specified. Some variables might only indirectly influence discretionary activities via their effect on another intervening factor.

Path Analysis

This book uses a statistical method called path analysis to develop a model of volunteering.[2] This method combines the results of a series of multiple regression equations and presents these results in a visual format. A major benefit of path analysis is that it allows for the interrelationships among all of the variables to be illustrated graphically and the relative importance of the factors to be expressed statistically. The direction of a relationship between two variables is shown by an arrow and the relative strength of several predictors of one dependent variable is possible by comparing the standardized beta coefficients which indicate the influence of the independent variable on the dependent variable.

Stepwise regression analysis was used to create the path model. In this method, the program selects, step by step, variables having the greatest influence on the dependent variable. The variable with the most predictive ability is selected in the first step, the second most powerful in the second step, and so on. When the independent variables specified in the program are no longer significant, the program ends itself. It is possible, using this procedure, to look carefully at how each variable is influenced by the independent variables and how each one makes a contribution to explaining the dependent variable. As will be clear when the path model itself is developed, this feature is an especially valuable one since it is important to develop a model that minimizes the numbers of variables included and, at the same time, maximizes the explanatory power.

Developing a Path Model of Volunteering

Predictors of Life Satisfaction, Activity, and Volunteering

Since life satisfaction and activity serve as intervening variables between volunteering and the social and demographic factors that influence it, table 10–1 presents the results of three regression analyses which predict these three variables as a first step in developing a path model.

Life Satisfaction. The first column indicates the predictors of life satisfaction. The strongest predictor is perceived health, a finding consistent with most previous research on this topic.[3] The next set of factors selected were education, income, and marital status. These three had about equal effects on life satisfaction. There is an inverse relationship between work deprivation and life satisfaction; older people who miss working more have lower life satisfaction scores. The last predictor of life satisfaction, which has the smallest influence, is religion: there are higher scores among Jews and Protestants. Overall, the predictive power of the model is high. All of the variables influence about 30 percent of the variance in life satisfaction. Most of this is due to the impact of health, which explains 25 percent of the variance.

Table 10–1

Results of Stepwise Multiple Regression Analysis Predicting Life Satisfaction, Activity, and Volunteer Status

(standardized beta weights)

Variable	LSIA	ACTIVITY	NOWVOL
PERHEALTH	.398	.174	
ACTIVITY			.257
LSIA		.205	.079
EDUCATION	.102	.267	.142
AGE	n.s.	− .088	− .073
INCOME	.112	n.s.	n.s.
MARR	.098	n.s.	n.s.
NWORK	− .069	n.s.	n.s.
RELIGION	.053	n.s.	n.s.
OCCUPATION	n.s.	n.s.	n.s.
GENDER	n.s.	n.s.	n.s.
WHITE	n.s.	n.s.	n.s.
WIDOW	n.s.	n.s.	n.s.
ALONE	n.s.	n.s.	n.s.
WORKS	n.s.	n.s.	n.s.
VOLRET	n.s.	n.s.	n.s.
Adjusted R^2	.304	.266	.158

n.s. = not significant.

Activity. According to data in the second column of table 10–1, a person's activity level is most influenced by educational achievement, which explains 16 percent of the variance. Older people with higher educational levels are more active. It is important to note, in this respect, that the two other indicators of socioeconomic status, income and occupation, do not influence activity. The second most important influence on activity is life satisfaction.

In contrast to earlier studies of activity and life satisfaction, this study uses life satisfaction to predict activity. This was done because an analysis using a statistical technique called LISREL showed that activity was influenced by life satisfaction. (See chapter 9.) The third influence on activity is perceived health. It is important to note that educational achievement has a far greater impact on older people's levels of social activity than either age or health. Age is a significant influence on activity but by itself adds less than 1 percent to the variance in activity after education, life satisfaction, and perceived health. A sizeable amount of the variance in activity, close to 25 percent, is explained by these variables.

Volunteering. The third column in table 10–1 shows the influence of these variables as predictors of whether or not a person is a volunteer (NOWVOL). The strongest influence on volunteering is a person's overall activity level. This finding led to the observation that volunteering was part of a generally higher activity level of some older people. The higher involvement of volunteers also extended to other formal organizations (such as senior centers and community centers), to higher interaction with friends, neighbors, and family, as well as to other types of leisure activities including going to the library and to restaurants. Three other factors predict volunteer participation—educational achievement, life satisfaction, and age. About 15 percent of the variance in NOWVOL is explained by the variables.

It is also important to consider some of the variables having a smaller effect than expected. Neither activity level, life satisfaction, nor volunteer status were affected by any of the measures of role loss (WIDOW, ALONE, VOLRET, or WORKS). Occupation and income had no impact on volunteer status or activity.

Determinants of Perceived Health, Education, and Income

A number of variables significantly associated with volunteering in earlier chapters (such as religion, gender, and race) might indirectly influence volunteering via their effects on other variables such as perceived health, education, income, and work deprivation. Table 10–2 shows the results of regression analyses performed in order to identify the possible indirect effects of some of these.

Effects of Race. This analysis was particularly important in understanding the impact of racial differences. Race does not directly affect volunteering but does have a significant impact on a person's educational achievement which then, in turn, influences whether or not a person is involved in doing volunteer work. Racial differences within the older population might primarily be the result of educational differences rather than a reflection of a distinctive life-style.

Table 10–2
Results of Stepwise Multiple Regression Analysis Predicting Perceived Health, Education, and Income
(standardized beta weights)

Variable	PERHEALTH	EDUCATION	INCOME
EDUCATION	.200		.342
AGE	n.s.	−.143	−.129
INCOME	.171		
RELIGION	n.s.	.110	
OCCUPATION	.070		.094
GENDER	n.s.	n.s.	.192
RACE	.091	.321	.089
MARR	n.s.		.185
Adjusted R^2	.163	.129	.361

n.s. = not significant.

Effects of Gender. The effect of gender on volunteering is also an indirect one. It mainly influences volunteering because older men and older women have different income levels in old age. This finding suggests a need for future research to examine whether some of the differences between older men and women that are often assumed to reflect different patterns of adjustment instead might mainly be the result of the lower incomes of older women.

Effects of Religion. Religious differences in volunteering are not great when other factors are taken into account. (See table 10–1.) There are two main reasons why religion might influence people's participation in volunteering. First, there are religious differences in educational achievement. (See column 2 of table 10–2.) Second, there are religious differences in levels of life satisfaction. (See column 1 of table 10–1.) Protestants and Jews had higher life satisfaction scores than Catholics.

A Path Model of Volunteering

The data in tables 10–1 and 10–2 were used to guide the development of a path model, figure 10–1. The model includes the variables having a significant impact on another variable. In order to maximize the explanatory power of the model and, at the same time, to only include variables that made a contribution to explaining the dependent variables in it, the model only includes variables whose addition to the model added at least 1 percent more to its ability to explain the variance of the dependent variable. Since the path diagram excludes some independent variables in the equations in tables 10–1 and 10–2, the path coefficients in the model are different from those in the two tables.

Effects of Role Loss

Two types of role loss (retirement and widowhood) have been the subject of a significant amount of research. This interest is understandable because they are the two most important status transitions in many older people's lives. The data in this book show, quite clearly, that role loss may not have as enduring an effect on older people's lives as often believed.

Retirement and widowhood did not lead to a greater tendency to be involved in doing volunteer work. With regard to retirement, this is evidently part of a larger pattern in which people do not greatly expand their leisure activities when they retire (see chapters 1, 3, and 8 for discussions of this), since activity levels were no higher when people theoretically had more time for leisure by virtue of not working. The only circumstance where volunteering was higher was for people who were semiretired; these people commonly combined a reduced work schedule with volunteering. Semiretirement was most

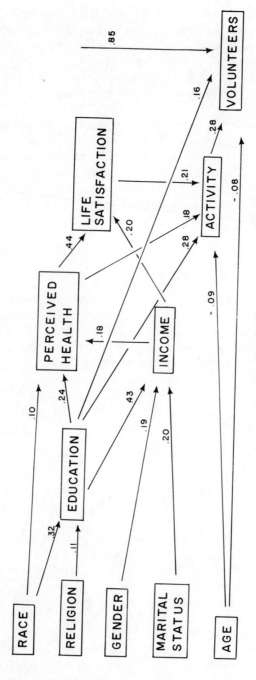

Figure 10–1. Path Model of Volunteering by the Elderly

often combined with volunteering by better-educated people who might have job skills that could be translated into volunteer work. This may be an example of how volunteers are a self-selected group of people who are able to work without pay because they tend to have higher levels of life satisfaction and have work-related skills that make them desirable volunteers.

Some recent research on the effects of retirement indicate that it does not have a strong impact on life satisfaction that is independent of the fact that retirees tend to be in less favorable health, are older, and have lower incomes than people who continue to work.[4] Similarly, changes in work and employment status were found to be less important predictors of levels of involvement in formal and informal activities than indicators of socioeconomic status.[5]

Work deprivation merits discussion since it has a different effect on people's life situations than was originally envisioned. The view of volunteering as a work-substitute suggested that there would be a positive relationship between work deprivation and volunteer status. That people do not compensate for the things they miss about working by volunteering was a surprising finding at first. A careful review of similar research revealed that people do not volunteer in order to compensate for the frustrations or lack of gratification from their jobs. When people retire, they do not use leisure as a way to compensate for the loss of work since the leisure activities that they select do not appear to fulfill the same attributes they enjoyed in their work.[6]

Work deprivation had a negative impact on life satisfaction; even though the effect was not great enough to be included in the model, the relationship does merit some consideration. A high score indicates that a person missed a greater number of features about working. Since retirement is an expected and normal part of growing old, this measure may actually be an indicator of well-being since a high score may mean that an older person has not yet come to terms with a usual transition of growing old in this society, the reduction or cessation of work.

The lack of associations between role loss, activity levels, and life satisfaction should not be interpreted to mean that retirement and widowhood are not major events in people's lives. The findings suggest something else: When other circumstances and characteristics of older people's lives are considered—their education, income, and perceived health—widowhood and retirement may have less enduring effects on various aspects of adjustment to old age than previously thought.

The only indicator of role loss included in the model is marital status; being unmarried has a negative impact on income. This is not a subjective effect of the loss of a spouse which is a result of widowhood, divorce, or separation, but reflects an objective change which then has an impact on people's levels of well-being.

Effects of Increasing Age and Declining Health

As people grow older, they tend to reduce their social activities and their involvement in doing volunteer work. It is clear that increasing age has an important effect on volunteering and that age influences volunteering independently of the fact that people might be physically less able to volunteer as they grow older. In comparison to other factors such as education, the effects of age were not strong; activity levels were much more influenced by life satisfaction and perceived health, neither of which were affected by age. This might initially seem to be a finding that is much at variance with what is generally observed to accompany increasing age.

These findings are understandable in view of two facts about the meaning of age. First, figures 4–1 and 4–2 show that a major decline in volunteering does not occur until relatively late in people's lives, close to the age of 80. A second important consideration is that the older population consists of people in several different generations, and the younger age groups are better educated. Age itself may not influence volunteering as much as the fact that increasing age is associated with lower educational achievement and also lower income. This is a confirmation of an observation first made by Cutler (see chapter 5) that what appear to be effects of age on voluntary association membership are sometimes actually due to lower socioeconomic status of older generations.

Changes in health have a major effect on older people's lives. Being in good health enables older people to carry on their usual activities and maintain their well-being. One of the very first studies of the positive effects of activity on life satisfaction noted the importance of good health on life satisfaction: "Relatively good health . . . increased the probability that *high* morale would be found even when activity was low."[7] It is often said, especially by older people, that if you have your health, you have everything. The path model shows that this is quite true. Perceived health is the most important predictor of life satisfaction, and it has a much greater impact on life satisfaction than income. Indeed, perceived health alone explains 25 percent of the variance in life satisfaction.

There is also a considerable amount of evidence, based on ethnographic studies of retirement communities, that a person's health has an impact on placement in age-segregated communities. People in poorer health are pitied by other older people.[8] By extension, being in excellent health places an older person in an envied position relative to others which, in turn, either improves or reinforces a higher level of well-being.

One relationship that was expected, but did not exist, was that increased age would be a major predictor of perceived health. There is a correlation between the two but, when other factors are considered, perceived health is not influenced by age and is, instead, influenced by education and income. This points to the central role of social status in the experience of growing older.

Effects of Education, Occupation, and Income

Educational achievement is the most powerful predictor of adjustment to old age. It has the strongest impact on volunteer status, and it is the most important determinant of activity level and of perceived health. There are various ways that educational differences can shape the experience of growing older. Education probably influences activity and volunteer status for several reasons. First, better-educated people are likely to have higher levels of "leisure competency."[9] This means that people with more education are more knowledgeable about the kinds of leisure activities available and probably have a wider range of interests.

An older person's current or former occupation and current income are much weaker predictors of activity levels than education. One of the most surprising findings (especially in view of much of the important research on how a person's occupation has an important impact on adjustment to retirement[10]) is that educational differences were so much more important for understanding activity levels than occupation (which is not in the model). What may have seemed to be occupational differences in adjustment to retirement may, instead, have been due to the educational differences of occupational groups. The lack of impact of income on activity may reflect the income-levelling effect of retirement, which means that income differences become less pronounced during old age.[11] A retired automobile worker could therefore have the same (or higher) income as a former college professor. (See chapter 5.)

Effects of Race, Religion, and Gender

The two chapters looking at these three ascribed status characteristics reached the conclusion that these factors merit consideration but, that in the case of gender, differences between men and women were generally not strong. What is important, instead, is that work and retirement appeared to have a different impact on men's and women's tendency to be involved in volunteering. For men, especially retired men, retirement is associated with a significant reduction in the tendency to volunteer. If volunteering serves as a work-substitute for any segment within the older population, it is for women who have retired from professional jobs. The regression analyses and the path model show that race and religion indirectly affected volunteering. The effects of race and religion must mainly be understood in the context of educational differences. For nonwhites and Catholics (and Hispanics, who are frequently both nonwhite and Catholic), this means that the lower level of involvement in volunteering is mainly a reflection of their lower educational achievement.

Older Volunteers as Joiners

Volunteering is part of a more general pattern of active social involvement which extends not only to belonging to formal organizations, as several earlier studies found, but also to being more involved in a variety of leisure activities including reading, going to the library, and visiting friends and family. The direction of the relationship between volunteering and life satisfaction is an interesting one; higher life satisfaction leads to higher activity. Volunteers probably do not have higher levels of life satisfaction because they are positively influenced by their volunteer work or by their social activities in general, but because people with higher levels of well-being tend to be the more active ones in old age.

It is quite likely that a process of self-selection may be operating and that it occurs on the part of volunteers and also by organizations. Organizations might select people who have higher levels of well-being and who have work skills and abilities which they can bring to their volunteer work. People with higher social standing tend to join organizations more often and also stay in them longer.[12]

Continuity of Health, Activity, and Life Satisfaction

This investigation initially focused on activity theory because it has influenced social programs for older people and perspectives on older volunteers. The analysis provided no evidence for the validity of that theory; volunteering did not serve as a substitute for the loss of work and family roles. Another finding, which does not confirm activity theory, is that life satisfaction influenced activity which in turn affected volunteering. Activity is an effect rather than a cause of life satisfaction. Volunteering is part of a more general style of active leisure.

It is valuable to interpret these findings from the perspective of another theory in social gerontology, continuity theory. This theory is useful in understanding why indicators of role loss had no effect on life satisfaction and leisure patterns of older people, and why high activity is an effect rather than a cause of life satisfaction.

Continuity Theory

Unlike two other major theories of aging (activity theory and disengagement theory, which view old age as a time of major change), continuity theory specifies that the patterns established in earlier periods of a person's life are major forces in determining behavior patterns during old age.

> In a sense, the self becomes institutionalized with the passage of time. Not only do certain personality processes become stabilized and provide continuity, but the individual builds around him a network of social relationships which he comes to depend on for emotional support and responsiveness and which maintain him in many subtle ways. It is from this point of view that the typical aging person may be said to become, with the passage of years, a socio-emotional

institution with an individuated structure of supports and interactional channels and with patterns which transcend many of the intrapsychic changes and losses that appear. . . . [A]s individuals age, they become increasingly like themselves.[13]

Some recent studies question whether retirement and widowhood actually have an enduring impact on well-being. It is also quite likely that a person's health, life satisfaction, and social participation show a significant amount of continuity over the course of people's lives. This perspective is a very appropriate one for understanding why some older people volunteer and others do not, why some factors—such as age and role loss—are less influential than might have been expected, and, finally, why volunteering is primarily a result of socioeconomic factors and is one facet of a more active life-style during old age.

In a summary of findings of the Duke Longitudinal Studies, Palmore observed:

> The best single predictor of a person's status, attitude, or activity was usually their score on that same variable at a previous point in time. Persons who were wealthier, healthier, more employed, more active, and more satisfied at the beginning of our studies tended to be wealthier, more employed, more active, and more satisfied at the end of our studies, despite all the age changes that took place.[14]

Health

It is generally assumed that one consequence of increasing age is that a person's health deteriorates. While this is, in general, quite true, the process may not be a linear set of changes on a year-by-year basis, which is captured by the kind of multiple regression techniques used here, but a large change at a certain point in one's life which results in a major decrease in a person's health.

It is quite clear that role losses do not have a strong impact on physical health. A recent major study on retirement, based on seven different longitudinal studies, reached the conclusion that "Retirement at the normal age has little or no adverse effects on health for the average retiree. Some have health declines, but these are balanced by those who enjoy health improvement."[15] One reason why role loss may not have a great impact is because people's health stays relatively constant over their lives.[16]

Life Satisfaction

Finally, several studies also indicate that life satisfaction is a fairly stable quality which is not greatly affected by external circumstances. Data from the most extensive panel study on older people, the Duke Longitudinal Study, indicated that there was a great deal of stability in a person's level of life satisfaction.

Very little change in people's scores was reported; significant changes in individual scores tended to balance each other out so that the overall picture was one of stability.[17] Life satisfaction also appears relatively unaffected by widowhood[18] and by retirement when other potentially confounding factors are taken into consideration.[19] The model here shows that perceived health and income influenced life satisfaction.

Social and Leisure Activities

There is also evidence for stability in patterns of social and leisure activity over the course of a person's life. Even though people might change some of their leisure activities as they grow older, a number of studies reviewed in chapter 1 show that there is indeed a good deal of continuity in people's activities and that role losses do not have as great an effect on some areas of social interaction as previously believed.[20] In fact, it is quite possible that people's levels of voluntary association membership may be significantly influenced by their parents' patterns[21] and that people who are joiners in old age were also joiners in middle age:

> "Joining" appears to be a relatively stable aspect of life style. This suggests that we are at least partly "prisoners" of past activity patterns, finding it difficult or unattractive to reorganize life styles which have been set much earlier in life. It also suggests that there may be few new or attractive associational options available to older people. Many voluntary associations are linked to the roles and activities of young adulthood and middle age; relatively few are geared to the interests and needs of older people.[22]

It is important to consider the impact of a person's past experiences in understanding reasons for participation or nonparticipation in volunteering and in many other social and leisure activities. The effects of previous experiences are strong as is the impact of educational achievement. In contrast, older people's lives may be less affected by retirement or by widowhood than previously thought.

Not All Activity Is Pleasurable

An implicit assumption in the view that various types of social activities enhance older people's well-being is the idea that activity, in and of itself, is good. Perhaps this original view reflects an important bias in American culture which older people have violated: that to be busy is good. This is, after all, a society in which the notion that "idle hands are the devil's work" is far stronger than a recent emphasis on being "laid back."

It is quite possible that formal social participation—in voluntary associations and in volunteering—might not always be positive and, in fact, could be damaging to older people with fragile egos. This is another explanation for why active older people might be a self-selected group with initially higher levels of life satisfaction. Several possible explanations why activity might not always be good have been offered. First, older people could be shunted aside in age-mixed organizations; thus, participation might not be valuable since the interesting and meaningful roles are given to younger members.[23] Even among their peers, systems of stratification among older people might not provide reinforcement for people with initially lower levels of life satisfaction and might, instead, provide opportunities where their less favorable situation compared to their peers might reduce their morale.[24] In this sense, people with limited social contacts might be adapting a viable life-style which permits them to maintain an existing level of well-being.

A third notion, which has clear-cut implications for recruitment of older volunteers and will be more extensively discussed in the next chapter, is that not all volunteer work may provide older people with positive experiences. Volunteering in a program designed especially for older people may have particular benefits. However, even in such a program, older people might compete with paid workers who view them as a threat to their jobs, especially in instances when retirees might have better work skills than paid workers.

Summary

Volunteering is part of a general leisure style of some older people. Older volunteers are more active in a variety of ways. High activity is a characteristic of people who are better educated and have higher levels of life satisfaction. It is quite likely that high activity is an effect rather than a cause of life satisfaction because individuals and organizations are engaged in a process of mutual self-selection. Organizations select older people with higher social status and higher levels of life satisfaction; older people with these qualities are also more active.

There is also a substantial amount of evidence that the variables that influence volunteering—activity, life satisfaction, and perceived health—are characteristics that are quite stable over the course of people's lives. Continuity theory is therefore a far more appropriate perspective for understanding volunteering by the elderly than activity theory. Data indicate then that volunteering by older people is much more clearly understood from the perspective of continuity theory than activity theory.

Notes

1. D.H. Smith, "Determinants of Individuals' Discretionary Use of Time," in D.H. Smith and J. Macaulay, eds., *Participation in Social and Political Activities* (San Francisco, Calif.: Jossey—Bass, 1980), pp. 36–37.

2. O.D. Duncan, "Path Analysis: Sociological Examples," *American Journal of Sociology,* 1966, Vol. 72, No. 1, pp. 1–16.

3. For a review of eighty-one studies exploring the relationship between these factors, see A. Zautra and A. Hempel, "Subjective Well-Being and Physical Health: A Narrative Literature Review with Suggestions for Future Research," *International Journal of Aging and Human Development,* 1984, Vol. 19, No. 2, pp. 95–110.

4. G.B. Thompson, "Work versus Leisure Roles: An Investigation of Morale among Employed and Retired Men," *Journal of Gerontology,* 1973, Vol. 28, No. 3, pp. 339–44.

5. Wan and Odell, op. cit.

6. See G.E. O'Brien, "Leisure Attributes and Retirement Satisfaction," *Journal of Applied Psychology,* 1981, Vol. 66, No. 3, pp. 371–84.

7. Maddox, op. cit., p. 203.

8. C.F. Longino and C.S. Kart, op. cit., p. 718.

9. T. Tedrick, "Leisure Competency: A Goal for Aging Americans in the 1980s," in Osgood, op. cit., pp. 315–18.

10. See Simpson and McKinney, op. cit., pp. 54–73.

11. Fillenbaum et al., 1985.

12. J.M. McPherson, "A Dynamic Model of Voluntary Affiliation," *Social Forces,* 1981, Vol. 59, No. 3, p. 719.

13. B. Neugarten, 1964, op. cit., p. 198.

14. Palmore, op. cit., p. 109.

15. E. Palmore, B. Burchett, G. Fillenbaum, L.K. George, and L. Wallman, *Retirement: Causes and Consequences* (New York: Springer, 1985), p. 167.

16. Wan, op. cit., p. 485.

17. Palmore, op. cit., p. 98.

18. Ibid., p. 100.

19. Palmore et al., 1985, op. cit., p. 167.

20. Wan and Odell, op. cit.

21. Hodge and Treiman, op. cit., pp. 730–31.

22. Ward, op. cit., p. 444.

23. Ibid.

24. Longino and Kart, op. cit., p. 718.

11
Consolidating and Expanding Volunteering by Older People

There are two types of older volunteers: people who have a history of volunteering over the course of their lives and people who begin to volunteer later in life. This chapter provides some perspectives and specific recommendations regarding the involvement of older people in volunteering and looks at this issue from two vantage points. First are some strategies that increase the chances that volunteers continue to participate as they grow older. Second are strategies to encourage others to either begin or resume their participation.

A number of the recommendations are based on the book's most important finding, that older volunteers probably have a long-standing history of participation. Volunteering is probably more consistent with earlier behavior and not greatly affected by the need to compensate for role loss. Continuity theory is a more useful perspective for understanding the meaning of volunteering in old age than is activity theory. Before turning to specific recommendations, a general discussion of some research on the subject of the motivations, recruitment, and retention of older volunteers is appropriate. It focuses on whether older people are influenced by very different motivations than people of other ages.

Perspectives on Volunteering

American society is mainly guided by secular values. In contrast to traditional societies where people did not retire and where older people were more closely tied to the social fabric because they lived in extended families, today's older people grew up and matured in a society emphasizing material success and individualism. Continuity of behavior must be understood in the context of American culture; the number of older volunteers is greatly limited by the facts that people tend to maintain the same behavior patterns throughout their lives and that the desire or the ability of people to change radically is quite small. It is perhaps unrealistic to expect that people who devoted their lives to their own private affairs will, because of widowhood or retirement, become more interested in public and communal matters.

Why Do Older People Volunteer?

There are a number of different reasons why people volunteer. The desire to compensate for the loss of work and family roles has been assumed to be an important one for older people. Yet, there is no strong evidence that this is true in either this book's study population or in others; people who are widowed or retired do not have a higher tendency to volunteer than people who are married or still working. Responses to questions on reasons for doing volunteer work also provide no indication that role loss is an important factor; the most common reason, which was given by almost one-quarter of the people questioned in a recent study sponsored by AARP, was the desire for self-fulfillment, an individualistic rather than altruistic motivation. Only a small proportion, 7 percent, viewed volunteering as a way to socialize with other people.[1] For some people, volunteering could also be a way to fill time. A study of the New York City Second Careers program found that this was a much more common motivation for retired men than for retired women.[2]

It is important to distinguish between the original reasons why a person begins to volunteer and the reasons for continuing. The few systematic studies on this question indicate that the motivations change over time. Once a person begins to volunteer, a desire to do "good deeds" declines and the nature of the volunteer job itself becomes more and more important.[3] People are more affected by the nature of the responsibilities, whether or not the situation is satisfying, and relationships with coworkers. A recent study of older volunteers in eleven agencies in Los Angeles outlined some of the features of volunteer work that contributed to their satisfaction and their continued participation. Three factors were highly correlated with satisfaction: receiving supervision, having increased responsibility, and receiving recognition. There was a higher level of satisfaction when volunteer jobs were structured like paid jobs.[4]

Are Older Volunteers Different?

A major question about older volunteers is whether or not they are initially guided by different motivations and, once involved, whether they have very different needs than people of other ages. The evidence on the subject is limited and suggests no clear-cut answer. Since the older population is a diverse group, it is difficult to generalize whether all older volunteers are different. There are, however, some unique experiences about growing older that should be borne in mind. Since there is no systematic study of differences between older and younger volunteers with regard to their motives, needs, desires, or performance, many of the points mentioned here are quite speculative.

As a group, older volunteers are members of different generations than younger volunteers. Their historical memories and their occupational and educational profiles are quite different. The current older population is a less-educated group with a less well developed sense of leisure competence than future generations are likely to have.

It is also important to keep in mind that the older population consists of members of several different generations. People now in their eighties were born at the turn of the century; those entering their sixties were born not long before the economic depression of the 1930s. The older population is a diverse group composed of people with different historical memories, educational profiles, religious affiliations, and leisure patterns.

Another aspect of growing older is that many older people have lost a major source of their identity and the basis for placement in the stratification system: an occupation. It is quite possible that most people's identities are not as closely bound to their occupations as was assumed in discussions of retirement as a "crisis."[5] Retirement may only be a crisis for some people but, regardless of whether or not it is, the loss of a work role inevitably involves the redefinition of a person's identity and a reorganization of time. For some people, it also can mean a significant loss of power and prestige.

A common assumption in discussions of older people's use of their time is that a high level of activity is beneficial. There is some evidence (see chapter 8) that voluntary association membership and volunteering do not always yield positive results. People with low self-esteem and limited interpersonal skills might place themselves in situations that could damage their egos rather than enhance their well-being. This can especially be true in situations involving members of several generations; these are not always positive experiences for older people because they can be shunted aside[6] or treated with a level of deference bordering on patronization.

A final difference is that older volunteers are not linked to volunteer jobs by work- and family-related ties. Retirees are not subject to the expectation that they should be involved in community service, which is a common motivation, especially for men. Family-related involvements are also less important than at earlier stages in life. These points are further confirmation of the fact that older volunteers are more influenced by the nature of the volunteer jobs they are given than are younger volunteers.

In many other ways, older volunteers are not so very different from people in other age groups. A well-designed volunteer program with features intended to meet the needs of individual volunteers might therefore attract and also retain older volunteers.

Recruitment of Volunteers

One of the consequences of living in a secular society is that organizations cannot rely on humanitarian values to ensure an adequate supply of volunteers.

It is therefore necessary to stimulate the existence of altruistic behavior by recruiting volunteers. Volunteer administrators recruit volunteers by appealing to altruism as well as to self-interest. There is a particular emphasis on the individual benefits; volunteering is presented as an enjoyable way to spend time and to learn new skills, not only as a way to serve others.

A number of different recruitment methods are used. Typically, organizations rely on a combination of them. Publicizing an organization's work in the mass media is a way to generate general interest and possibly new volunteers. Organizations locate new volunteers through voluntary action centers, some of which can be specially designed to recruit and place older volunteers.

A third method, which volunteer administrators view as being the most effective, is direct solicitation: asking people if they can give their time.[7] This approach is viewed to be effective for several reasons. It identifies people who, once recruited and trained, have a greater chance of continuing to work, offer appropriate jobs skills, and enjoy the ability to adapt well to a work situation.

Deciding to volunteer is a two-step process. In the first stage, a person becomes aware of an organization's need for volunteers. There is a gap in time between becoming aware of an opportunity and actually making a commitment; the transformation of vague interests and intentions into an actual commitment requires what has been called a "trigger event"—an occurrence that somehow crystallizes a general desire into a more tangible set of actions. In a study of March of Dimes volunteers, the trigger event usually involved another person, often a friend (52 percent), neighbor (20 percent), or coworker (18 percent).[8] This same conclusion was reached in a more recent study conducted in Great Britain.[9]

A survey of seventy-one volunteer administrators suggested several ways to institutionalize trigger events. One way is to use informants within a community who can identify volunteers. These "nominees" can then be invited to an informal meeting. These techniques point out the need for a person's services and the interpersonal relationships that can be cultivated in the course of doing volunteer work. These methods have been borrowed from the field of community organization where they were used to expand citizen participation. In the field of volunteer administration, they are appropriate for increasing a different form of social involvement—working as a volunteer in a formal organization.[10] Direct recruitment methods probably locate people who are already joiners since they are the most likely to be identified. As will be discussed later, it is important that nonjoiners who might have the desire to modify their usual behavior be identified in this way.

A second direct recruitment technique is to have volunteers identify and recruit others. This has been used by a number of programs. A Retired Senior Volunteer Program in Tuscaloosa, Alabama, called this approach the "be one, reach one" campaign.[11]

Many organizations have successfully used the mass media to locate new volunteers. This approach has the major advantage of casting a wider net than direct recruitment by individuals or the identification of potential volunteers by informants. It is the most effective way to locate people with a limited amount of experience as volunteers. However, it can turn up a higher ratio of people who might be inappropriate for the available positions than other methods might.[12]

Organizations also locate new volunteers through voluntary action centers. Some of these centers refer people of all ages while others mainly focus on older people. Several studies done in Great Britain have systematically considered the kinds of people who are referred by them. It found that "volunteer bureaus" tend to refer people who are quite different from most volunteers; they mainly appeal to new volunteers, particularly younger women, and do not often place people from working class backgrounds.[13] It would be valuable to consider whether older volunteers who make use of centralized referral bureaus are new volunteers or if they are people with a history of participation who go to these organizations to find new "jobs."

Retention of Older Volunteers

Volunteering is an exchange; individuals work without pay, possibly alongside other people who get paid for doing similar jobs. In return, volunteers reap certain benefits. They can receive prestige from their status as a volunteer, which for some people could be an important part of their identity in retirement. This motivation is reinforced by publicly identifying oneself as a volunteer by carrying a tote bag or wearing a medal indicating recognition for a specific amount of service.

Since it is time-consuming to train new volunteers, organizations have a strong incentive to retain current volunteers. A major problem for all jobs, including volunteer jobs, is that people become burned out.[14] Organizations can adopt various procedures designed to reduce burnout. Rewarding volunteers, almost from the moment of initial contact, is extremely important in maintaining a highly committed work force.

A major problem for volunteers of all ages, including older volunteers, is that they tend to be underutilized by being assigned to jobs that do not use their skills and abilities.[15] Many professionals are unable to make use of volunteers in an effective fashion. A study of social workers' attitudes toward volunteers illustrates some of the problems inherent in staff–volunteer relationships. The professionals believed that volunteers were most useful when they were in clerical jobs and were least useful as group leaders or providers of direct services to clients. Staff felt more at ease with two types of volunteers: teenagers and older people.[16] Both types could, perhaps, be more easily subordinated than "adults" in their middle years.

The underutilization and possible subordination of volunteers of all ages merits closer study. Several reasons account for this situation. Very few professionals are trained to work with volunteers. There are several other sources of strain. Volunteers can impinge upon the turf of professionals and are viewed as threatening to the job security of paid workers.[17] These factors contribute to the underutilization of volunteers' skills and possibly an unnecessary degree of subordination to paid workers.

Two articles point out that burnout is more common among enthusiastic volunteers who were in leadership positions. This is described as being due to limitations of the volunteers: they lack skills and have unrealistic goals.[18] The articles fail to point out another reason for burnout, that the most enthusiastic volunteers might be unwilling to accept the underutilization of their skills and an unnecessary subordination to paid workers.

Older volunteers probably face a unique set of problems when they perform the same kinds of tasks they once did as paid workers. An early discussion of some of the benefits of volunteering indicated that retired social workers had a great deal to offer social agencies.[19] The use of a person's skills increases the potential satisfaction of the volunteer.[20] At the same time, it means that an organization has an experienced worker at no cost. However, retirees might be more skillful than paid workers, or they might *think* they are more skillful— another possibility with a different set of problems. Very little is known about the relative success and failure of assigning retirees to positions that draw upon their work skills or whether it is more effective to place them in situations that require them to develop new skills. The use of older people in volunteer jobs in their former occupations is an area with a number of possible sources of tension and conflict.

Recommendations

Expanding participation of older people involves two very distinct processes. First is increasing or redirecting the efforts of people who already volunteer. The first three recommendations below address that issue. A second approach is to expand participation by those who, without specific efforts, would probably not be involved in volunteering; the fourth through sixth recommendations are applicable to them. The seventh and eighth recommendations are appropriate for consolidating and also for expanding participation. The final recommendation concerns maintaining individuals' participation.

1. Expand Participation by Joiners

The strongest direct influence on volunteering is a person's general activity level. Older volunteers are more active in a variety of ways: they go to senior centers and community centers; they go to movies, restaurants and libraries; and they spend more time with friends, neighbors, and family. Volunteering is part of a more general pattern of active involvement during old age. Since the people who are volunteers tend to be joiners, the most efficient recruitment methods will involve locating new volunteers where they tend to go—churches, libraries, senior centers, and other types of organizations.

2. Present Volunteering as an Option
in Preretirement Planning Programs

Many preretirement planning programs commonly include a component that discusses volunteering as an interesting way to spend time. It is important to realize, however, that only a small minority of retirees actually have some formal retirement preparation. Only one in ten in this book's study population who were fully retired had in fact taken such a course. (Most commonly, these were people who had been in managerial and clerical jobs.) Consolidation and expansion of participation among the newly retired is an especially important strategy. New retirees are easier to train than those who have been out of the labor force for a longer time.[21] Perhaps people who take a longer time to identify ways to spend time in retirement find this transition more difficult and adapt less well to a new role.

Some important differences between the ways men and women adapt to retirement might affect their volunteer patterns. Among the early participants in New York City's Second Careers Program, the women tended to volunteer much sooner after retirement than the men.[22] It is also striking that many men volunteered because of their wives' encouragement.[23] Retired professional women in this study population were more likely than men to use volunteering as a work-substitute. The impact of gender on the process of growing older is not well understood and probably has some important implications for the general subject of leisure and the more specific issue of volunteering.

3. Describe Volunteering as a Way to Achieve Self-
Actualization Rather than as a Form of Unpaid Work

American culture emphasizes the importance of working. At the same time, there is a common view that any job worth doing is a job worth getting paid for. This is probably a strong barrier to volunteering in all age groups, but as yet its impact has not been systematically considered. For some people— those who are joiners—volunteering should not be presented as a type of unpaid work but as a way to meet new people, to do some worthwhile and interesting things, and to learn.

4. Recruit the Less-Active Elderly by Using
the Mass Media

One characteristic of people who do not volunteer is that they spend relatively more time in solitary and inactive pursuits. They tend to watch television and listen to the radio more often than others. At the present time, the mass media are used to inform older people about the benefits of volunteering and the kinds of positions they can fill. These data confirm that this is an appropriate way to stimulate the interest of less-active elderly who tend to spend more time watching television and listening to the radio.

Research on public service announcements provides some insight into the best ways to communicate information with older people. The studies show that a variety of communication media can be used—newspapers, radio, and television. What appears to matter most is not the medium used but the selection of specific television or radio programs, newspapers, or magazines that have an older audience.[24]

One of the major difficulties in using publicity to identify new volunteers is that it may locate people who are inappropriate for the jobs at hand. Turning away volunteers can be detrimental to individuals and damaging to an organization's reputation. When organizations make use of extensive publicity, they must be prepared to place a variety of types of people or be able to assist them to find other positions.

5. Design Volunteer Jobs That Reduce the Negative Impact of Low Education and Retirement on Participation

The strongest predictor of volunteering is a high level of involvement in a variety of social activities. People who are more educated, in better health, younger, and more active are more frequently volunteers. It is difficult to determine whether some groups have relatively low levels of participation because people choose not to volunteer or if organizations have filtered them out and select people with different characteristics. Organizations can only increase the participation of a group with a limited level of involvement by modifying a variety of policies and procedures and by also designing new roles for volunteers. There are a number of special incentives for older volunteers: transportation, reimbursement for travel, free lunches, and small stipends. Another way to consolidate and expand the involvement of older volunteers is to be certain that there are appropriate jobs for people who might be in poor health.

6. Expand Participation by the Inactive by Emphasizing That Volunteering Is a Work-Substitute

There is an inverse relationship between volunteering and work deprivation. People who miss working more are actually less likely to volunteer. When this relationship was considered in the path analysis (chapter 10), it was clear that high work deprivation led to a low level of life satisfaction which, in turn, influenced a person's activity level. Perhaps volunteering could become attractive to some older people if they view it as a work-substitute. If viewed as unpaid work, some older people who have not come to terms with the loss of a work role might find volunteering to be a way to compensate for not working. The belief that any meaningful work merits payment might be an important barrier to their participation; this bias should be addressed when people are explicitly recruited to volunteer as a way of compensating for the loss of a work role.

7. Increase Participation by Intervening at Critical Points in the Life Cycle

There are several critical points in the life cycle when people are likely to stop participating in volunteer work and when new volunteers could also be recruited. One point is at the time of retirement itself. Although it is not possible to conclude that retirement is a reason for reduced involvement in volunteering, there is a strong relationship between lower participation and being retired in some subgroups in the older population, especially for men who have completely retired from professional jobs.

Retirement might be associated with a reduction in involvement for several reasons. Retirees tend to reduce their activity levels and spend more time in passive pursuits. Many people, especially men, volunteer for work-related reasons and these end when a person retires. It is important to maintain involvement at the point of retirement to counteract weakened expectations since it is a major turning point in people's lives.

Another critical point comes in people's late seventies when a reduction in volunteering occurs irrespective of perceived health. (See figure 4–2.) Comparisons with the findings of other studies suggest that the reduction in volunteering might be part of a shift in activity in general. The most valuable strategy for counteracting this tendency is to design volunteer jobs that can continue to be meaningful as people age and their health declines or to design special jobs for people in poor health.

8. Develop Programs That Link Older People to Volunteer Jobs Where They Have a Connection to the Social Roles They Occupy

One of the most successful programs for older volunteers has been the Foster Grandparents program. It has created a meaningful volunteer job which draws upon a set of skills and abilities possessed by people with different educational levels—the ability to provide emotional support to a child who suffers from a lack of positive interpersonal relationships. It is interesting that a meaningful family role which many older people occupy, that of grandparent, has never been explored as a way to link older people to organizations.

Organizations serving young people—such as scouting organizations, schools, community centers, little leagues—usually turn to parents as a source of volunteers. In the past, some of these jobs were filled by full-time homemakers. This traditional source of volunteers, women who are available during daytime hours to work with young people, is diminishing as an increasing number of women are in the paid labor force. Parents in their thirties and forties have limited amounts of time to volunteer since many combine work and family responsibilities. Grandparents—real ones in this case—are logical sources of assistance in schools, community centers, and scouting groups. Organizations should also elicit participation of grandparents at the same time they routinely recruit parents.

Many organizations have been quite successful in recruiting volunteers from the places where they work. This is viewed as a particularly efficient way to recruit men. Nonprofit organizations and community groups might forge alliances with companies to recruit people who have retired from them. This might serve to continue a tradition of community service among some workers into the retirement years.

9. Create Lateral and Vertical Mobility to Prevent Burnout

The continuity of involvement of volunteers of all ages, but particularly for older volunteers who lack the work- and family-related motivations, is highly contingent upon their assignment to appropriate and interesting jobs. A major task of volunteer administrators is to properly match the abilities and needs of volunteers with the demands of the jobs to be filled. As in paid jobs, people may benefit from changes in responsibility. Another way to consolidate participation and increase continuity is to create career ladders for older volunteers.[25] This could be done within an organization by promoting volunteers to new jobs, redefining their jobs, or routinely reassigning people to different jobs.

Conclusion

Volunteering is part of a more general pattern of adjustment to old age. The people who would be expected to have more time to be involved in doing volunteer work—homemakers and people who are completely retired—are less often involved in doing volunteer work than the people who should, in theory, have less time because they continue to work. The strongest predictor of a person's volunteer status is his or her level of involvement in a variety of social and leisure activities. Volunteering appears to be part of a general pattern which is less influenced by certain objective factors—how much time people have, how healthy they are—and more by the ways they choose to spend their time.

Certain demographic trends suggest that the number and proportion of older people engaged in volunteering should continue to increase. In the future, the older population will be a better-educated group, and more of it will be composed of women who are retired (rather than homemakers), a group who tend to be especially likely to volunteer. Current population projections suggest that a smaller segment of the older population will be foreign-born.[26] Those born outside of the United States will most often be Hispanics (whose participation levels are currently low) and Asians.

In addition to the potential impact of volunteering on older people's lives, there are at least two reasons why older volunteers will continue to be an important labor source. First, they are available during daytime hours. They fill a significant shortage by filling the jobs that used to be occupied by full-time homemakers. Second, older people will have more to offer organizations since they will be a better-educated group with a higher level of work skills. These qualities might also mean that older people will require different kinds of recruitment, jobs, supervision, and rewards.

This book has addressed an important issue facing American society and older people themselves: how people can construct lives with meaning in the absence of significant work and family involvements. Volunteering has been described as an important way to fashion a meaningful life-style in old age. It is likely that, under current circumstances, it mainly serves this function for a small segment of the older population: a self-selected group of older people with high life satisfaction and a history of successful involvement as volunteers over the course of their lives. An expansion in the numbers and types of volunteers requires attention to several areas: recruiting new volunteers, redirecting volunteers as they grow old, and showing sensitivity to the fact that the retention of older volunteers is closely linked to their levels of job satisfaction.

Notes

1. *Older Americans and . . . Volunteerism*, Program Department fact sheet (Washington, D.C.: American Association of Retired Persons, n.d.).

2. J. Stone and E. Velmans, "Retirees as Volunteers: Evaluation of their Attitudes and Outlook," *Volunteer Administration*, 1980, Vol. 13, No. 4, p. 6.

3. J.L. Pearce, "Participation in Voluntary Associations: How Membership in a Formal Organization Changes the Rewards of Participation," in D.H. Smith (ed.), *International Perspectives on Voluntary Action Research* (Washington, D.C.: University Press of America, 1983). See also M. Phillips, "Motivation and Expectation in Successful Volunteerism," *Journal of Voluntary Action Research*, 1982, Vol. 11, Nos. 2 and 3, pp. 123–24.

4. B.H. Kaplan, "Role Continuity in the Older Volunteer Role," *Dissertation Abstracts International*, 1978, Vol. 38, p. 7564-A.

5. R.C. Atchley, "Retirement and Leisure Participation: Continuity or Crisis," *The Gerontologist*, 1971, Vol. 11, p. 15.

6. Ward, op. cit., p. 444.

7. S.M. Chambré, "Recruiting and Retaining Minority Volunteers: A Qualitative Study of Organizations' Experiences," *Journal of Volunteer Administration*, 1982, Vol. 11, No. 1, p. 6.

8. D. Sills, *The Volunteers* (Glencoe, Ill.: Free Press, 1957), p. 102.

9. B. Mostyn, "The Meaning of Voluntary Work: A Qualitative Investigation," in S. Hatch, ed., *Volunteers: Patterns, Meanings, and Motives* (London, Great Britain: Cylinder Press, 1983), p. 30.

10. Chambré, 1982, op. cit., p. 6.

11. A.B. Heath, "The Retired Senior Volunteer Program," in Lorin Baumhover and J. Dechow, eds., *Handbook of American Aging Programs* (Westport, Conn., Greenwood Press, 1977), p. 86.

12. Chambré, 1982, op. cit, p. 8.

13. I. Mocroft, "Volunteers through Volunteer Bureaux," in S. Hatch, ed., op. cit., pp. 20–21.

14. See L.S. Dean, "Learning about Volunteer Burnout (It Can Improve Your Retention Rate)" *Voluntary Action Leadership*, Winter 1985, pp. 17–19. D. Hill, "How to Prevent Volunteer Burnout: An Interview with Martha Bramhill," *Voluntary Action Leadership*, Winter 1985, pp. 20–23.

15. J.P. Saxon and H.W. Sawyer, "A Systematic Approach for Volunteer Assignment and Retention," *The Journal of Volunteer Administration*, 1984, Vol. 2, p. 39.

16. F.S. Schwartz, "Training a Professional Staff to Work with the Program Volunteer," *Volunteer Administration*, 1977, Vol. 10, No. 1, p. 10.

17. L.L. Graff, "Considering the Many Facets of Volunteer/Union Relations," *Voluntary Action Leadership*, Summer 1984, pp. 16–20.

18. Heath, op. cit., p. 18. Hill, op. cit., p. 21.

19. Einstein, op. cit.

20. Kaplan, op. cit.

21. J.W. Freund, "The Meaning of Volunteer Services in the Schools: To the Educator and to the Older Adult," *The Gerontologist*, 1971, Vol. 11, No. 3, p. 207.

22. Stone and Velmans, op. cit., p. 5.

23. Interview with Fran Kleinman, director, Second Careers Program, Mayor's Voluntary Action Center, New York City.

24. R.M. Durand, D.L. Klemmack, L.L. Roff, and J.L. Taylor, "Communicating with the Elderly: Reach of Television and Magazines," *Psychological Reports*, 1980, Vol. 46, pp. 1235–42.

25. J. Sugarman, "RSVP in New York City: A Study of Volunteer Impact and Opportunity," paper presented at the Gerontological Society of America Meeting, Boston, Mass., November 1982.

26. P. Uhlenberg, "Changing Structure of the Older Population of the USA during the Twentieth Century," *The Gerontologist*, 1977, Vol. 17, No. 3, pp. 197–202.

Appendix:
Description of Variables Used in
Multiple Regression Analysis

Name	Description
NOWVOL	1 = current volunteer 0 = not a volunteer
ACTIVITY	An index using fourteen items in which respondents were asked about the frequency of engaging in fourteen activities. For most of them, six choices were possible. The score is equal to the total sum for all items divided by the number of questions that were answered.
LSIA	An eighteen-item scale measuring life satisfaction
WIDOW	1 = widowed 0 = not widowed
MARR	1 = married 0 = not married
ALONE	1 = living alone 0 = not living alone
WORKS	1 = working 0 = not working
RETIRED	1 = retired 0 = not retired
VOLRET	1 = retired voluntarily 0 = retired involuntarily
TYPERET	1 = semiretired 0 = fully retired
NWORK	A seven-item scale measuring work deprivation
AGE	Respondent's age
PERHEALTH	A seven-point scale measuring perceived health
GENDER	1 = male 0 = female
EDUCATION	Nine categories of educational achievement
INCOME	Fifteen categories of yearly household income

Name	*Description*
OCCUPATION	Nine categories of current or former occupation
RACE	1 = white 0 = nonwhite
RELIGION	1 = Protestant or Jewish 0 = Catholic

Index

ACTION, 4–5, 25, 28, 61
Activity level: and education, 105,
111; and health, 88, 105, 111; of
homemakers, 87–89; and income,
111; and life satisfaction, 92–95,
97, 98–99, 105, 112; and occupation, 111; and retirement, 29–30,
87–90; and volunteering, 5, 88,
105–106, 111–112, 122–123; and
work, 29–30, 87–90
Activity theory, 21, 30, 91, 92, 112,
117
Activity variable, predictors of, 105
Adams, D., 19
Age: and life satisfaction, 97; and
social participation, 34–35, 114;
and volunteering, 2, 5, 18, 19, 37,
51–52, 110, 113
Age and health: and socioeconomic,
status, 51–52, 110; and volunteering, 38–40, 51–52, 110
Aged population: age groups within,
28, 36, 40, 41, 47, 60, 66–67,
125; and androgyny, 56, 57;
black/white attitudes toward, 75;
and church attendance, 72; defined,
16; energy level decline in, 37; and
generational differences in amount
of leisure time, 7–8; and "gesellschaft"/"gemeinschaft" adjustment
patterns, 57; and income-leveling
effect, 45, 48, 75, 111; and indicators of social position, 47–48;
and intergenerational relationships,
91–92; living alone, 22; men/
women volunteers, 59–60; and
poverty, 75; racial differences in,

75–76; size of, 1; volunteers, 2;
women in, 59
Aging in the Eighties (Harris and
Associates), 16
American Association of Retired Per-
sons (AARP), 45, 48, 118
Americans Volunteer (U.S. Labor
Dept.), 58, 59, 72
Androgyny, 56, 57
Asians, 127
Atlanta study, 36

Black men/women volunteers, 78
Black/white women volunteers, 78–79
Blacks/whites (*see also* Race): attitudes toward older people, 75; and
economic status, 75; and education, 77, 106; and extended family
support, 75; and leisure time, 76;
and occupational groups, 77; and
religious/secular group participation, 76; and retirement, 75; and
social integration, 75; and socioeconomic status, 76, 77; and volunteering, 77–79; and widowhood, 75
Blue collar workers, skilled, and volunteering, 51, 61, 63
Blue collar workers, unskilled, and
volunteering, 77
"Burnout," 64, 121–122, 126

Canadian study, 95
Catholics, and volunteering, 72, 73,
78, 111
Church attendance, 72, 73, 74
Clerical workers, and volunteering,
51, 61, 63

About the Author

Susan Maizel Chambré is an assistant professor of sociology at Bernard M. Baruch College of the City University of New York. Dr. Chambré received a B.A. in sociology from Queens College, CUNY, and the A.M. and Ph.D. degrees from the University of Pennsylvania. She has also done research on patterns of welfare use by adolescent mothers and on ways to recruit black and Hispanic volunteers.